Brick Stitch, Peyote,

and Other Bead-Weaving Techniques

ACKNOWLEDGMENTS

The author would like to thank Perles & Co. for supplying all the materials used to make the jewelry in this book.

PERLES & CO

Find the author, Lucie Fossemalle, on her website:
thecamelia-bijoux.com

 Brick Stitch, Peyote, and Other Bead-Weaving Techniques is a translation of the 2019 version originally published by Fleurus Editions under the title *Brick-Stitch, peyote et autres techniques de tissages de perles* in France. This version is published by Fox Chapel Publishing Company, Inc.

ISBN 978-1-4971-0585-0

Library of Congress Control Number: 2025944956

To learn more about the other great books from Fox Chapel Publishing, or to find a retailer near you, call toll-free at 800-457-9112 or visit us at www.FoxChapelPublishing.com.
We are always looking for talented authors.
To submit an idea, please send a brief inquiry to acquisitions@foxchapelpublishing.com.
Or write to:
Fox Chapel Publishing
903 Square Street
Mount Joy, PA 17552

Printed in China
First printing

MIX
Paper | Supporting responsible forestry
FSC® C147414

Brick Stitch, Peyote,

and Other Bead-Weaving Techniques

LUCIE FOSSEMALLE

FOX CHAPEL
PUBLISHING

Contents

68

72

76

Introduction

Hi, I'm Lucie. I'm 23 years old, and I'm the creator of The Camelia Bijoux jewelry brand and editor of the DIY blog *The Camelia*. I've always loved creating things. When I was little, I loved drawing, cutting, assembling, gluing . . . and as soon as I was old enough to create something other than modeling clay ice creams and clumsy coloring book creations, I turned to jewelry design. Over time, my designs have become more and more accomplished. When my girlfriends would ask me where I got my jewelry, I could proudly say "I made it!" I started selling my jewelry at the age of 11, and I haven't stopped since. Today, I create jewelry that combines fine gold-plated brass and traditional Moroccan embroidery—a blend of tradition and modernity.

Besides creating my designs, I also enjoy sharing my expertise and ideas through my DIY blog and books, and by hosting creative workshops. I strive to make even the most complex designs accessible to everyone through my tutorials. I truly believe that anyone can create things with their own two hands!

In 2015, I discovered bead weaving, and "fell in love" with Miyuki beads. I was instantly drawn to the different weaving techniques that can be used to create a wide variety of bracelets, pendants, and earrings. This book brings together five different techniques to help you get started or improve your skills.

So, grab yourself some beads, get settled, and start weaving!

Lucie Fossemalle

Tools and Materials

All the jewelry in this book is made using Miyuki Delica 11/0 beads. These tiny seed beads, originally from Japan, are perfectly cylindrical and allow up to five strands of thread to pass through them. Thanks to their quality, the resulting weave is fine and uniform. These beads come in a wide range of colors and are sold in 5- or 8-gram packs. An 8-gram pack contains around 1,400 beads. You won't need that much for the projects in this book; for example, around 260 beads are used for Bird on a Perch Necklace (page 64).

1. Jewelry pliers: cutting (left) and chain nose (right)
2. Extra-strong glue
3. Bead loom
4. Hoop ear wires with crimp closures
5. French hook ear wires
6. Lobster clasps, 10mm
7. Jump rings: medium (Ø = 5mm) and small (Ø = 2–3mm)
8. Fine chain
9. Beading thread: Ø = 0.25mm (I use C-LON and One-G)
10. Beading needle
11. Nylon thread (for loom):

    Ø = 0.25mm for warp threads (stretched on the loom)

    Ø = 0.1mm for the weft threads (passed through the needle and threaded onto the beads)
12. Brass wire (Ø = 0.3mm)
13. Miyuki Delica 11/0 beads

Weaving Techniques

Cross Weave

This weaving is done freehand (without a loom) using brass wire, the ends of which cross inside the beads. This technique does not allow for very elaborate shapes, but rather simple ones like rectangles, triangles, and diamonds.

Peyote Stitch

Peyote weaving is done freehand, with rows offset from each other. The technique varies slightly at the end of the row, based on whether your selected number of beads at the start is even or odd. When it comes to circular peyote weaving, which allows you to weave a bracelet without adding a clasp, the end-of-row technique is also different for even- and odd-count peyotes.

Brick Stitch

Brick weaving is done freehand, with rows offset from each other much like a brick wall (hence the name). In this technique, the thread passes through each bead twice, making the weave stronger. This weave is particularly suitable for patterns featuring diagonals, triangles, and chevrons.

Loom Weaving

This technique uses stretched warp threads to form the structure of the weave, resulting in straight lines. The beads are then threaded onto a weft thread and woven between these stretched threads. They are, therefore, perfectly aligned.

Jewelry Assembly: Jump Rings

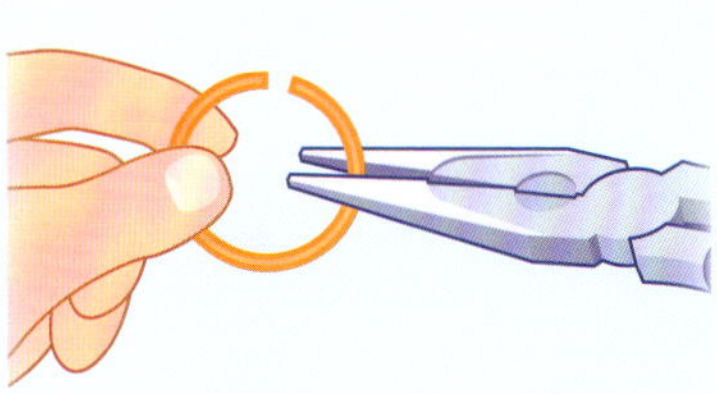

1. Place the ring with the slot facing upward. Hold it with your fingers on one side and the chain-nose pliers on the other.

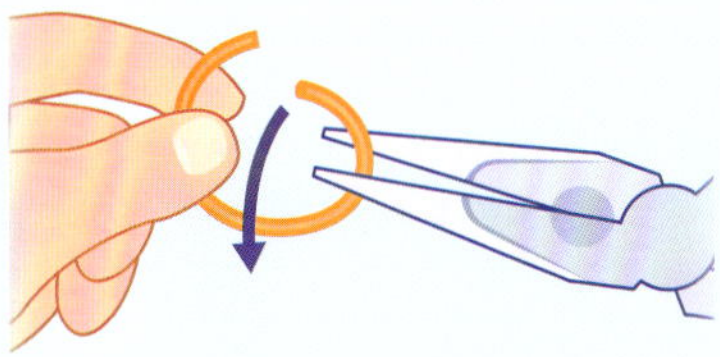

2. Open the ring by rotating one end toward you and the other in the opposite direction. Twist; do not open like a book.

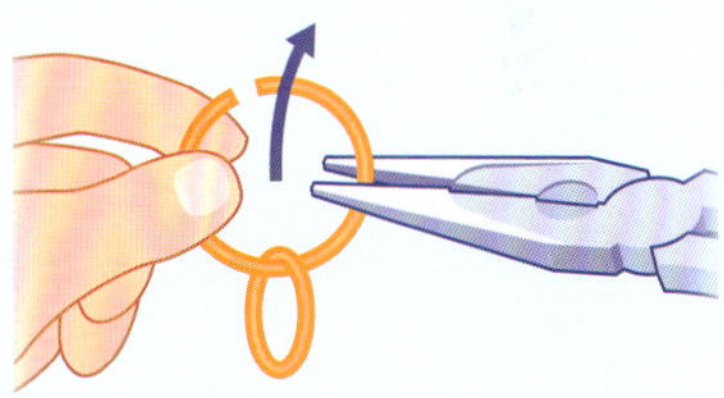

3. To close it again after inserting a clasp ring or other fastener, take hold of it as in step 1. Bring the ends together until it is closed.

CROSS-WEAVE TECHNIQUE

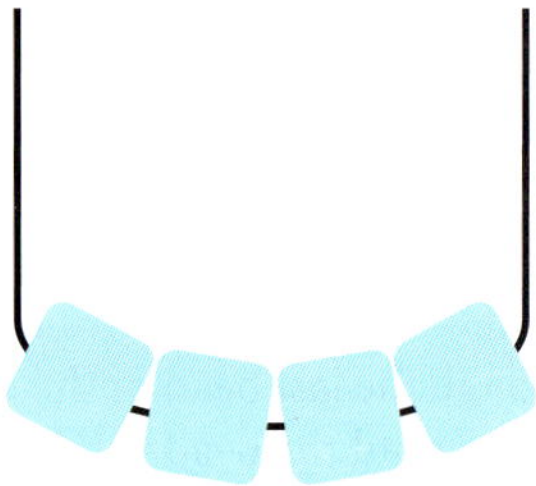

1. On the brass wire, pick up the beads for the first row. Form a U with the wire, so half of the wire is on the right and half on the left.

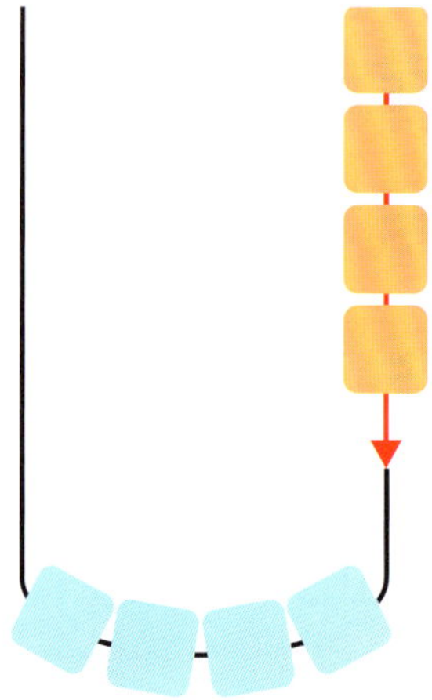

2. Pick up the beads for the second row onto the right wire.

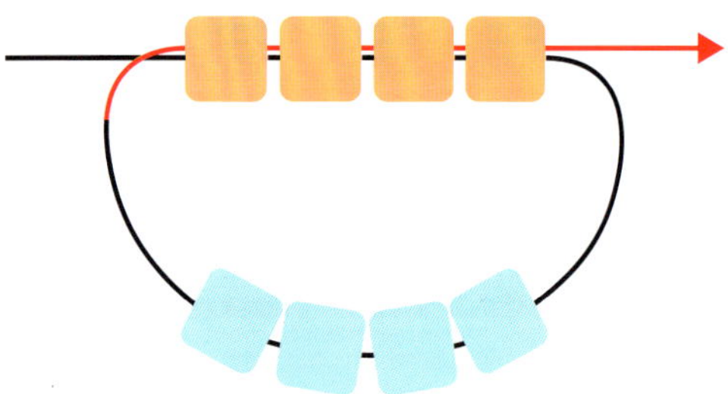

3. Pass the left wire through the beads on the right wire, so that the wires cross inside the beads.

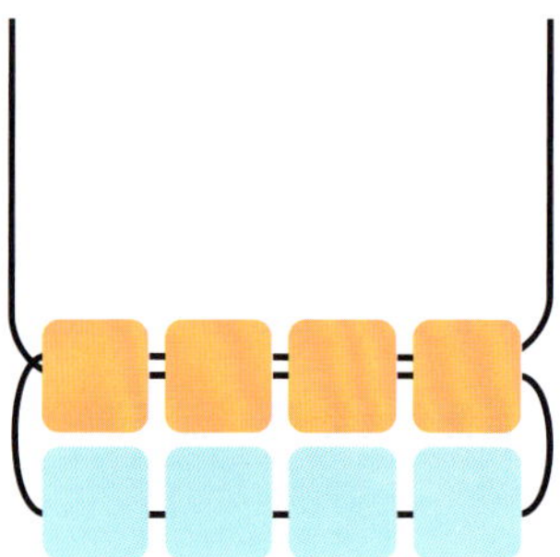

4. Tighten by pulling evenly on both wire ends so that the beads sit well.

EVEN-COUNT PEYOTE STITCH

1. Using a needle, pick up the beads that will form the first row (blue) and the second row (orange) alternately onto the thread. Slide them to the end of the thread.

2. Pick up the first bead for the third row (#7) and then pass it through the last bead of the second row (#5). Tighten the thread until the bead is positioned correctly.

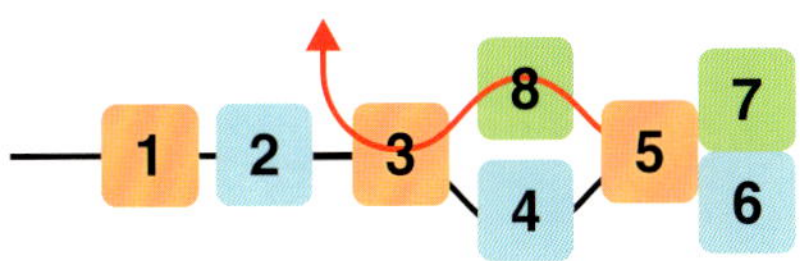

3. Pick up the second bead for the third row (#8), then pass the needle through bead #3. Bead #4 is skipped.

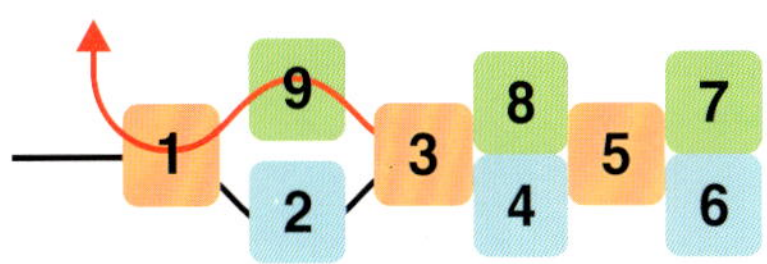

4. Repeat step 3 to add bead #9.

5. Follow steps 2–4 to add the fourth row (yellow), but one row above and from left to right.

6. To finish, pass the needle through the woven beads in a random zigzag pattern. Apply a dot of glue to the thread. Once the glue is dry, cut the thread flush with the bead.

ODD-COUNT PEYOTE STITCH

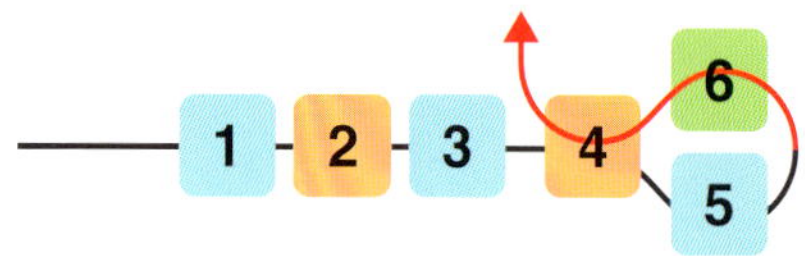

1. Using a needle, pick up the beads that will form the first row (blue) and the second row (orange) alternately onto the thread. Slide them to the end of the thread.

2. Pick up the first bead for the third row (#6), then pass it through the last bead of the second row (#4). Tighten the thread until the bead is positioned correctly. Continue the row as shown in steps 3–4 of Even-Count Peyote Stitch (page 11).

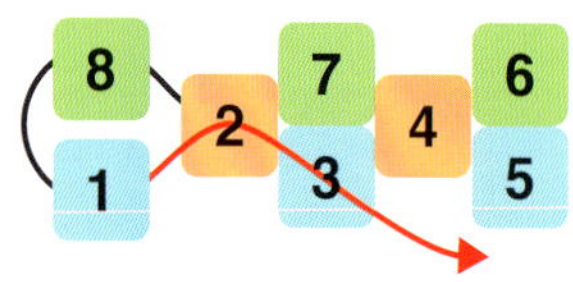

3. At the end of the third row (green), pass the needle through the first bead on the first row (#1).

4. Pass the needle diagonally through beads #2 and #3.

5. Pass the needle diagonally through beads #7, #2, and #1.

6. Pass the needle back through the last bead on the third row (#8).

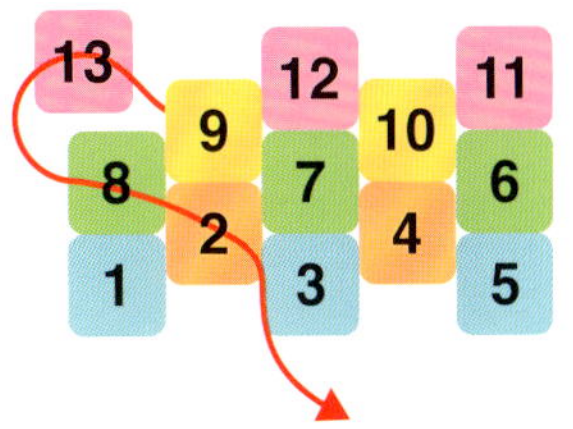

7. Weave the fourth (yellow) and fifth (pink) rows as before. When you reach the end of the fifth row, pass the needle diagonally through beads #8 and #2.

8. Pass the needle diagonally through beads #9 and #8.

9. Pass the needle back through the last bead on the fifth row (#13). This technique should be used at the end of each odd row.

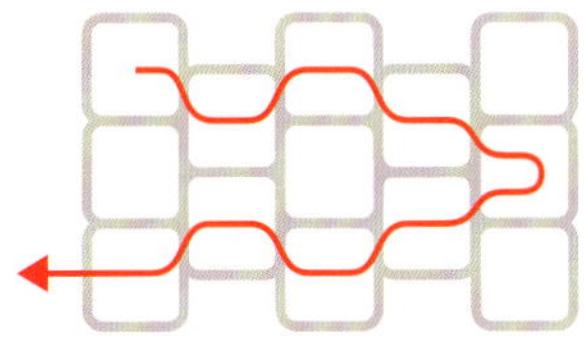

10. To finish, pass the needle through the woven beads in a random zigzag pattern. Apply a dot of glue to the thread. Once the glue is dry, cut the thread flush with the bead.

Decreasing for Even or Odd Peyote

1. Continuing from step 9 of Odd-Count Peyote Stitch, pass the needle through bead #9 and bring it out through bead #12.

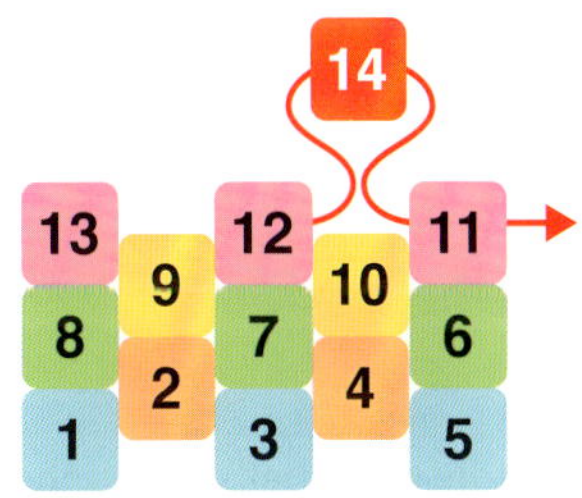

2. Pick up a new bead (#14) and pass the needle through bead #11. Depending on your pattern, continue the row as normal or repeat the decrease, symmetrically, at the end of the row.

CIRCULAR PEYOTE STITCH

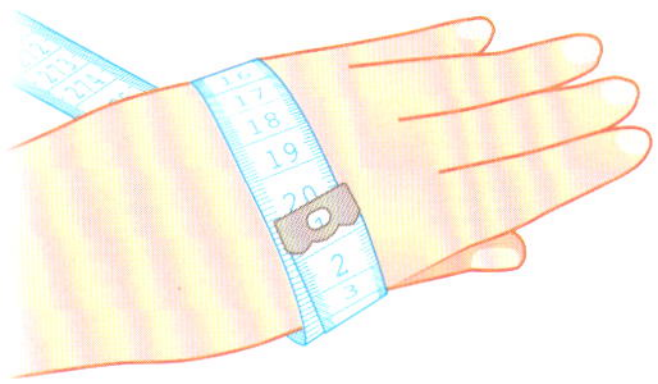

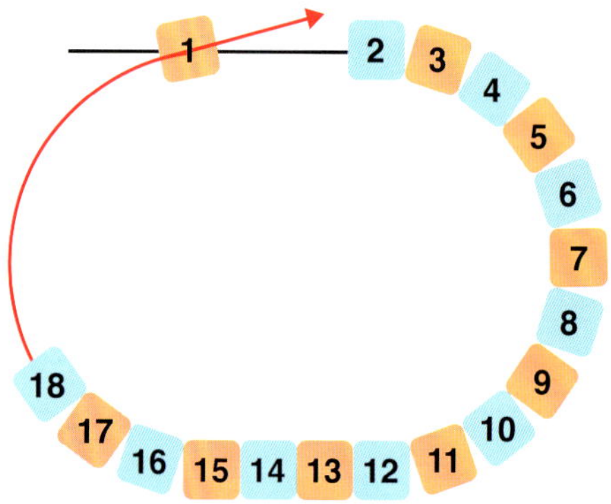

1. Circular peyote allows you to weave a bracelet without a clasp; therefore, it must be adapted to the size of your hand. Measure the circumference of your hand at its widest point (the connection point between your fingers and palm). Remember to fold your thumb inward as you would when putting on a bracelet without a clasp. This measurement is the length of your bracelet.

2. Cut a long thread. Using a needle, pick up the beads for the first (blue) and second (orange) rows, starting with a second-row bead and alternating until you reach the required length. The total number of beads must be even. (Here, I'm using a small number of beads to illustrate.) Pass the needle and thread back through the first bead.

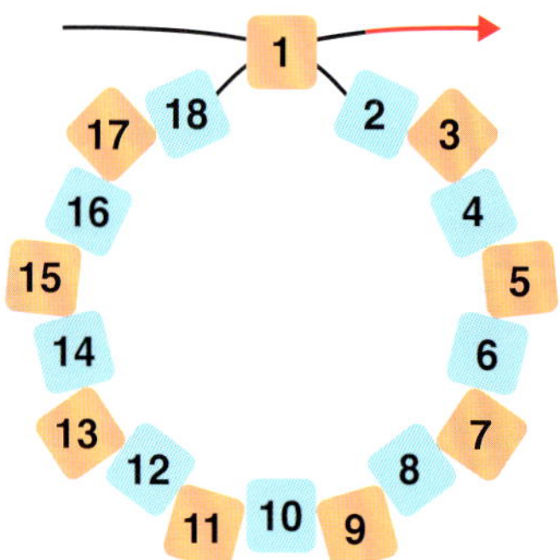

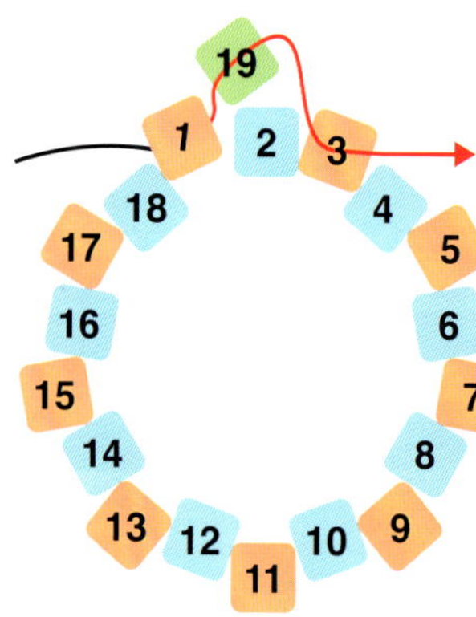

3. Pull the thread to the opposite side so the circle is formed. The first and second rows of the bracelet are now completed. The beads will naturally fall into place in a staggered pattern as you weave.

4. Start the third row (green) as an even-count peyote: pick up a new bead (#19), then pass the thread through the second bead in the second row (#3), skipping the first bead in the first row (#2).

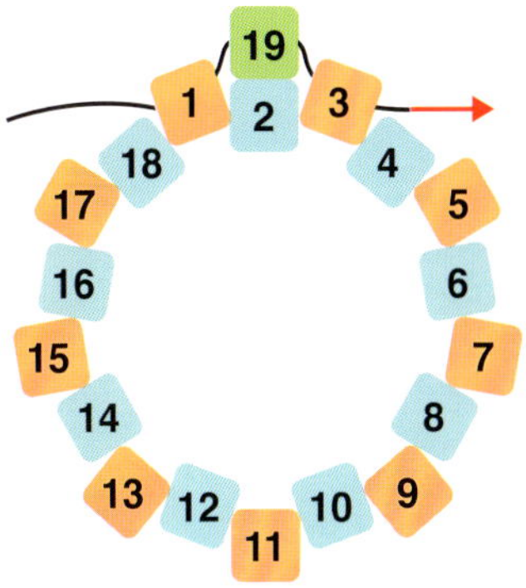

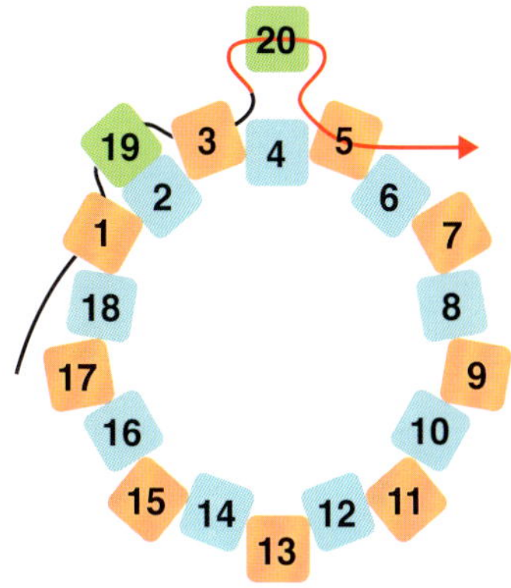

5. Tighten the thread until the bead is positioned correctly.

6. Continue weaving, always skipping one bead and passing the thread through the next. Tighten after each bead is placed.

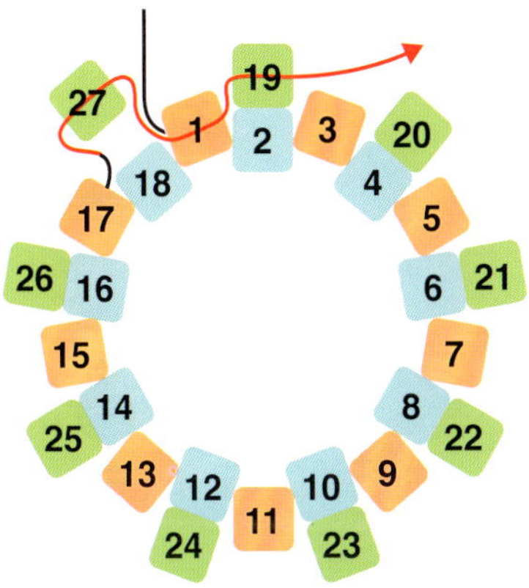

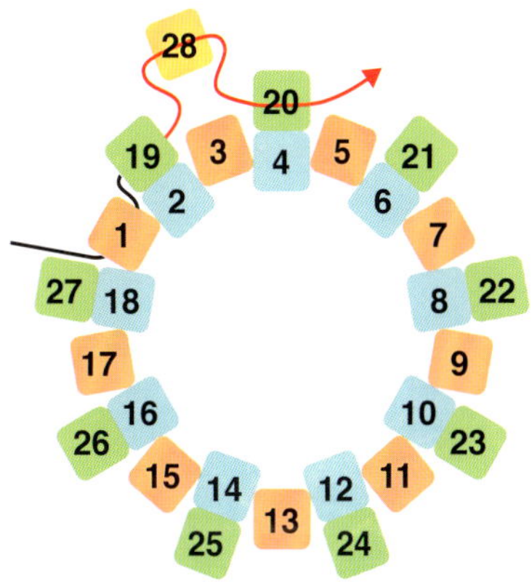

7. Pick up the last third-row bead, pass the thread through the first bead in the second row (#1), then pass through the first bead in the third row (#19).

8. Start and continue the fourth row (yellow), following steps 4–6. Continue with as many rows as desired.

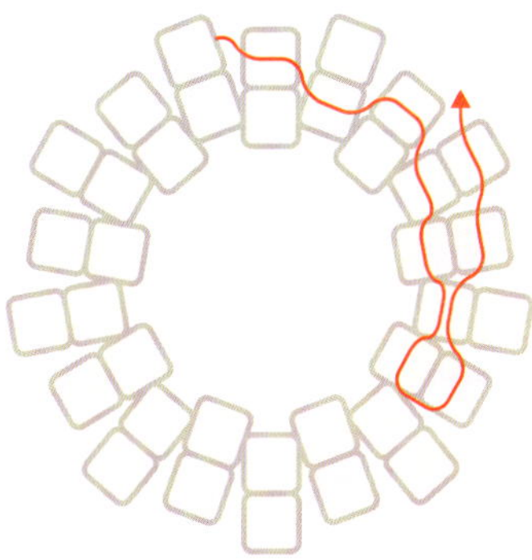

9. To finish, pass the needle through the woven beads in a random zigzag pattern. Apply a dot of glue to the thread. Once the glue is dry, cut the thread flush with the bead.

BRICK STITCH

For each of the jewelry patterns in this book that use brick stitch, the diagrams have an arrow indicating where you should start weaving for a more solid base. This is where the weave is widest.

Example Diagram

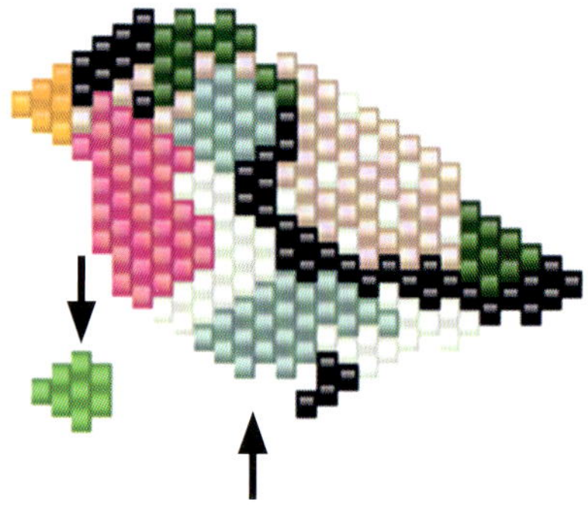

First Row

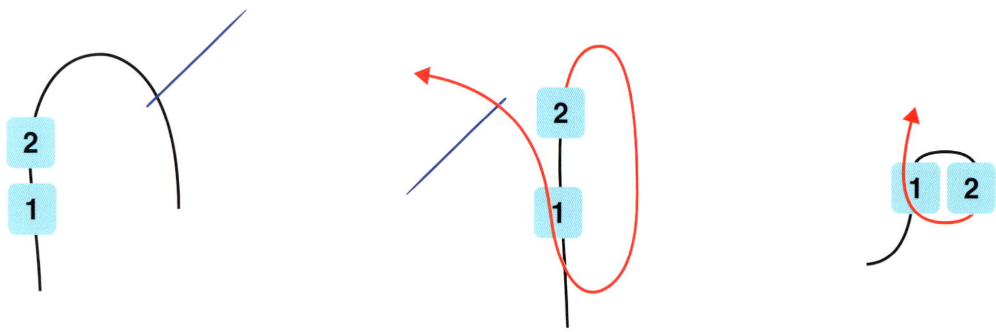

1. Pick up the first two beads using the needle and slide them to the end of the thread.

2. Pass the needle back through bead #1.

3. Tighten so that the two beads sit side by side.

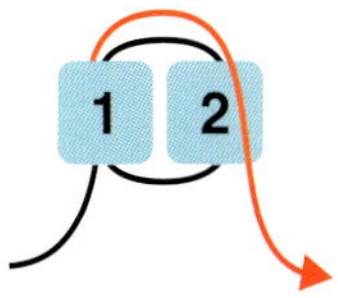

4. Pass the needle back through bead #2.

5. Continue the row by picking up a third bead.

6. Pass the needle back through bead #2 and out through #3.

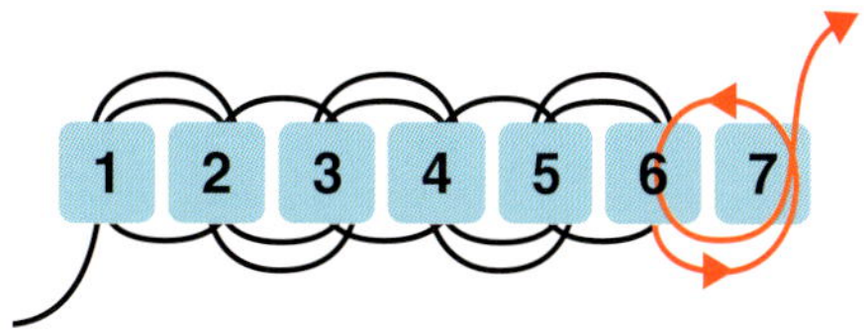

7. Repeat for the entire first row.

Starting the Second Row

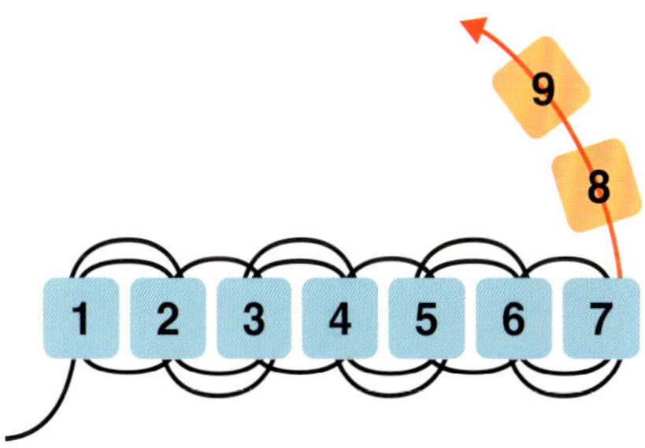

1. Pick up two new beads (#8 and #9).

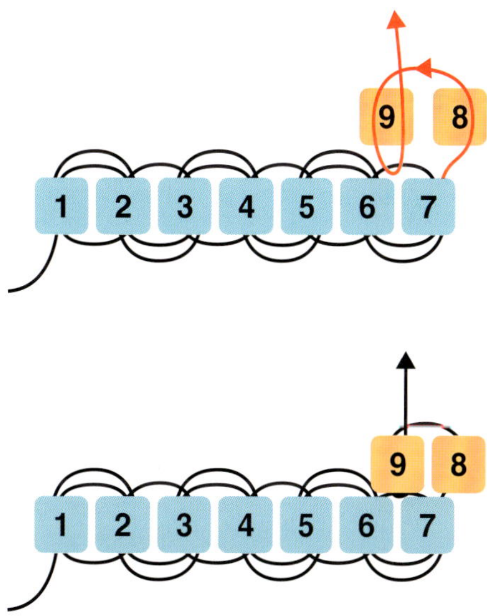

2. Slide the needle under the thread bridge that joins the two beads at the end of the first row (#6 and #7). Tighten until beads #8 and #9 are in place, then pass the needle back through the bead #9. Tighten the thread again.

Continuing the Brick Stitch

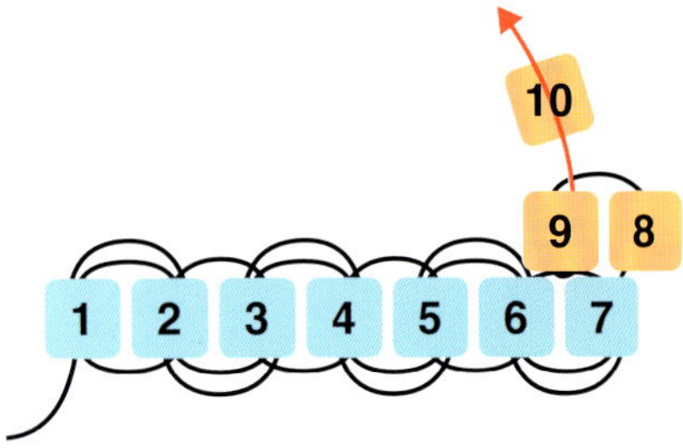

1. Pick up a new bead (#10).

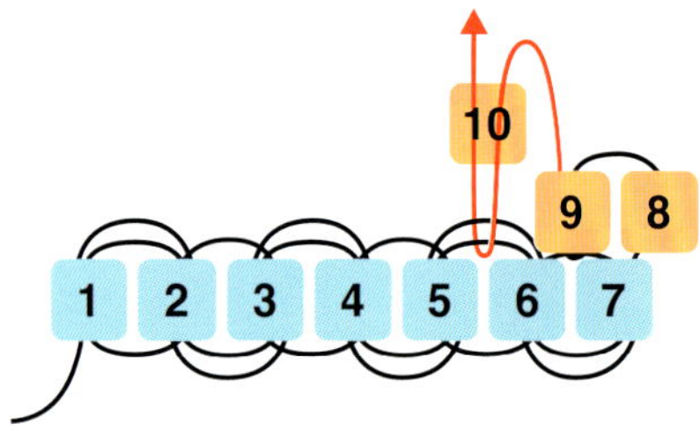

2. Slide the needle under the thread bridge that joins two beads on the row below (#5 and #6). Tighten until the bead is in place, then then pass the needle back through bead #10.

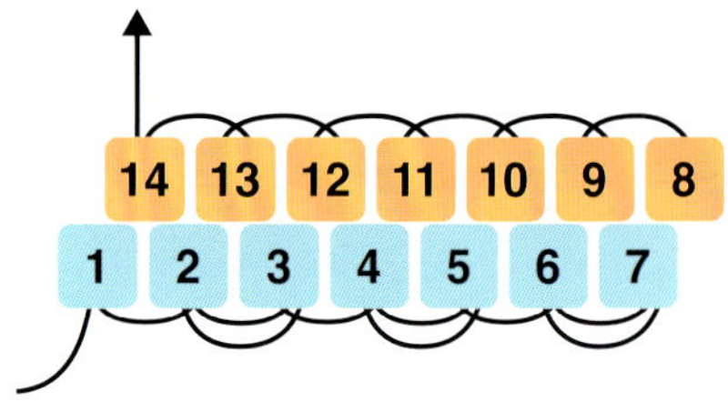

3. Continue in the same way until you reach the end of the row (once you have the same number of beads as the first row).

End-of-Row Increase

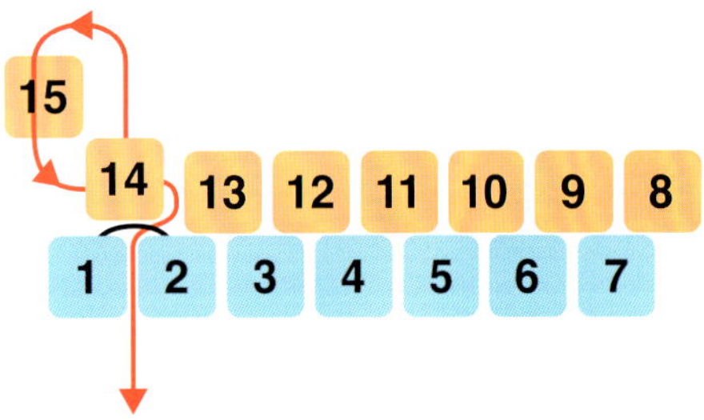

1. To increase the weave when you reach the end of the row, pick up a bead (#15). Pass the needle behind the previous bead (#14) to slide the needle under the thread bridge that joins beads #1 and #2.

2. Tighten the thread until bead #15 is in place. Pass the needle back through bead #15. Do not loop the thread around bead #1; use the technique shown in step 2 of Continuing the Brick Stitch.

End-of-Row Decrease

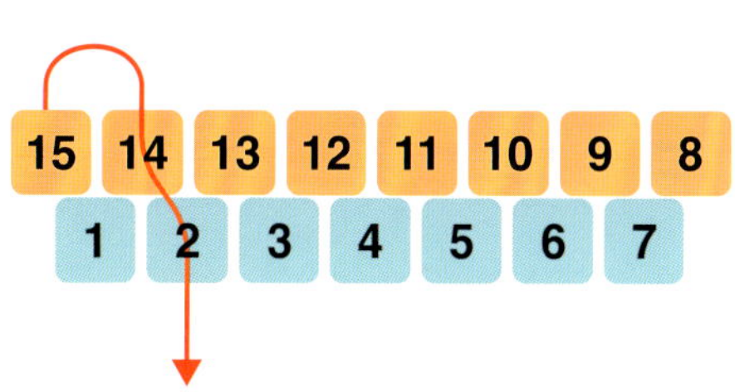

1. Pass the needle diagonally through the second-from-the-left beads in the previous two woven rows (#14 and #2).

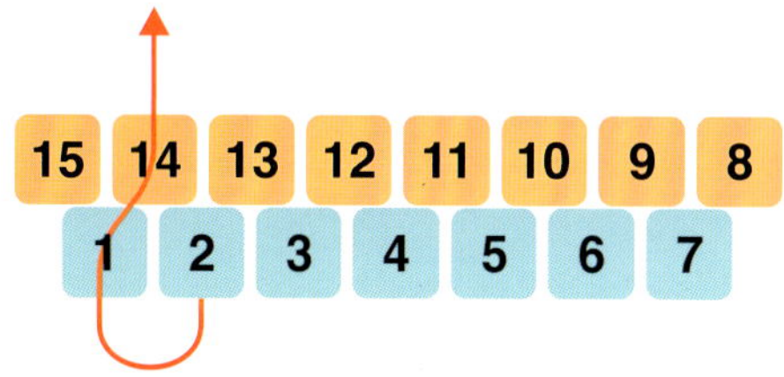

2. Pass the needle back through the first bead in the first row (#1), up from the bottom, and then through the second-to-last bead in the second row (#14), making a triangle shape you pass the needle through the beads.

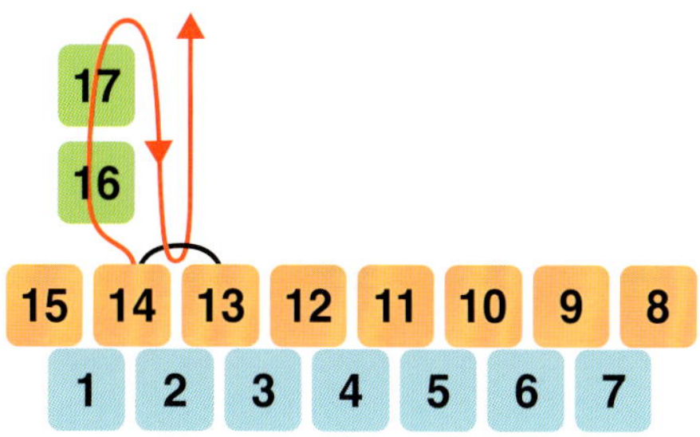

3. Pick up two beads (#16 and #17), then pass the needle under the thread bridge that joins beads #14 and #13 in the row below, from left to right. Tighten the thread until the beads are positioned correctly.

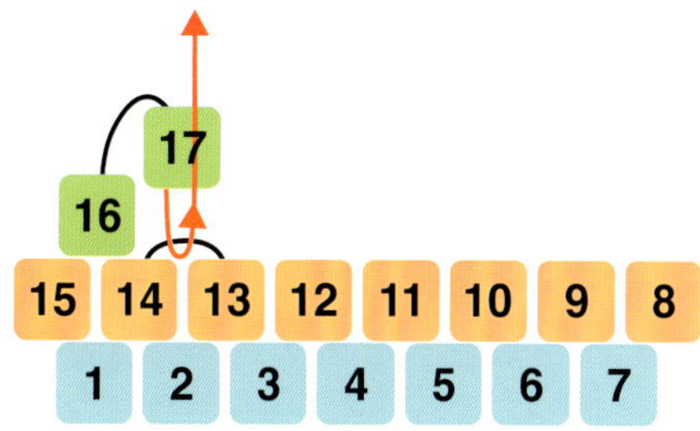

4. Pass the needle back through the new bead on the right (#17).

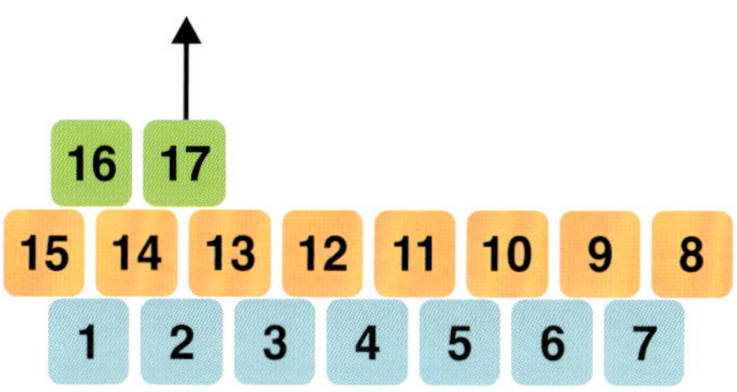

5. Tighten the thread until the bead is positioned correctly, then continue weaving as before.

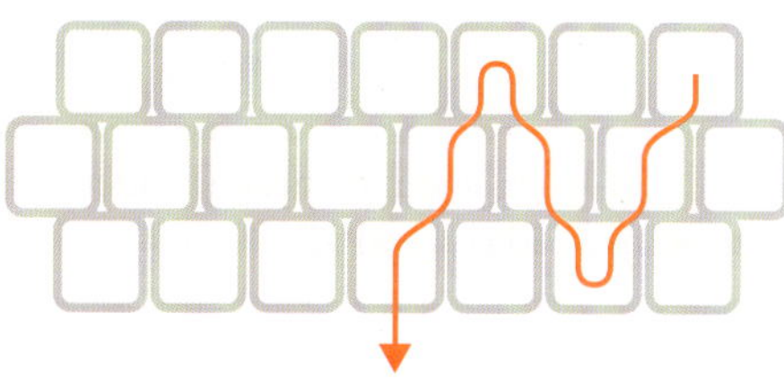

6. To finish, pass the needle through the woven beads in a random zigzag pattern. Apply a dot of glue to the thread. Once the glue is dry, cut the thread flush with the bead.

LOOM TECHNIQUE

Basic Weave

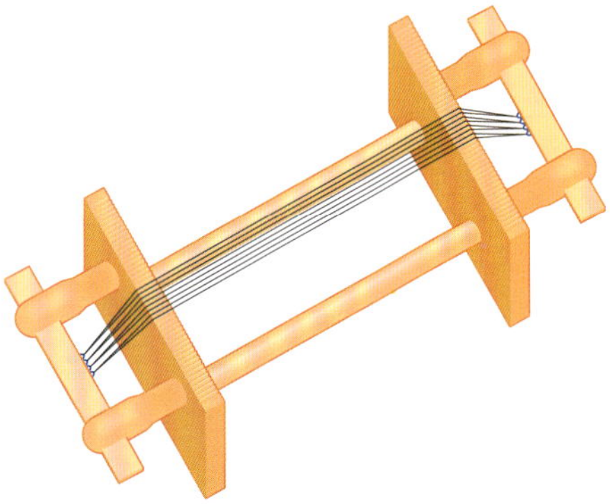

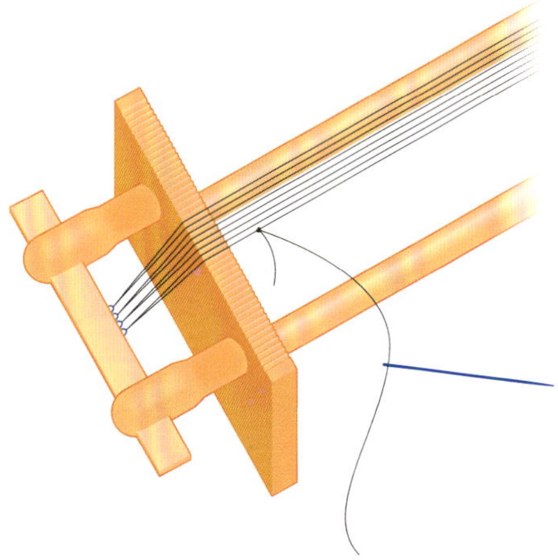

1. Attach and stretch 0.25mm nylon thread on the loom (warp threads). Always attach one row of thread more than the number of bead rows; for example, if you are weaving seven rows of beads, you will need eight rows of thread.

2. Tie the end of a long piece of 0.1mm nylon thread (for example, approximately 6½ feet [2m] for a bracelet) to the first warp thread, leaving 2" (5.1cm) of thread before the knot. This is called the weft thread. Thread its other end onto a needle.

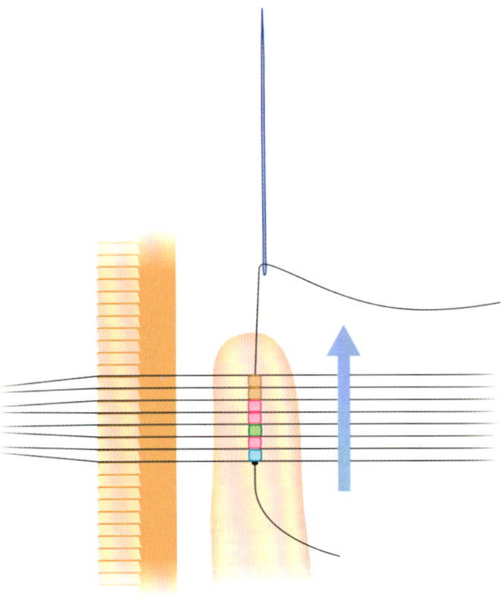

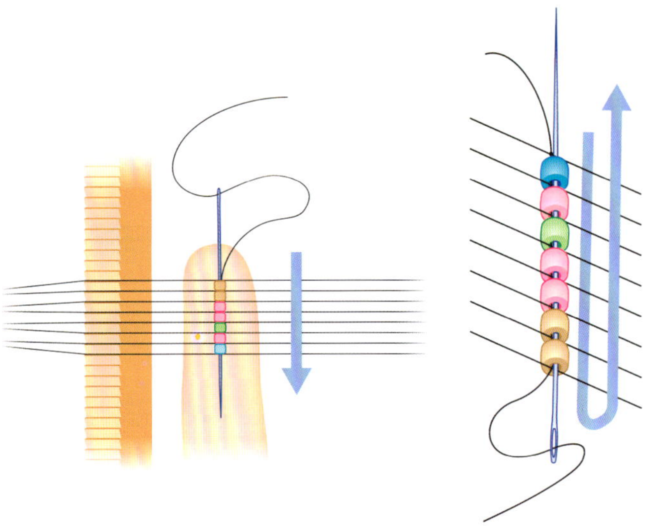

3. Pick up the first row of beads onto the needle, following the pattern in the diagram, and slide them to the starting knot. Pass the thread under all the warp threads, gently pushing the beads with your left index finger (if you are right-handed) to position them between the threads. Each space should contain a bead. Hold them firmly.

4. Lift the beads slightly with your finger. Pass the needle over the warp threads and back through all the beads from top to bottom, locking them in place. Tighten the thread until they are fixed and align them using your finger. Repeat steps 3–4 for the remaining rows until the grid pattern is complete.

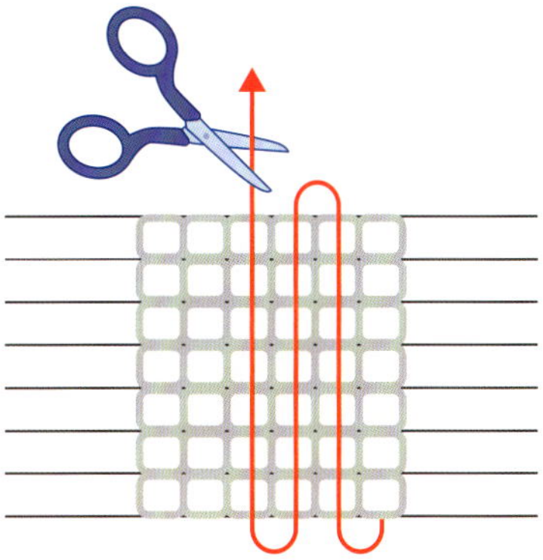

5. To finish off your weave, pass the thread back through the previous rows in a zigzag pattern. Cut it flush with the bead.

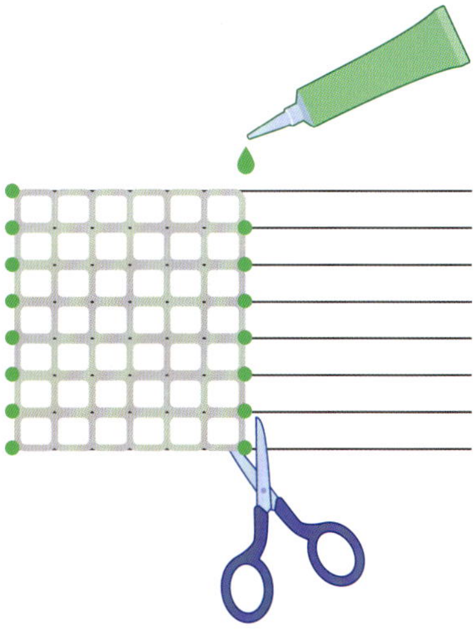

6. Apply dots of glue to the side of each end bead on the warp threads. Once the glue is dry, remove the weave from the loom and cut the excess warp threads flush with the weave.

Important Note!

In each row, the thread runs back and forth through the beads, first *under* then *over* the warp threads.

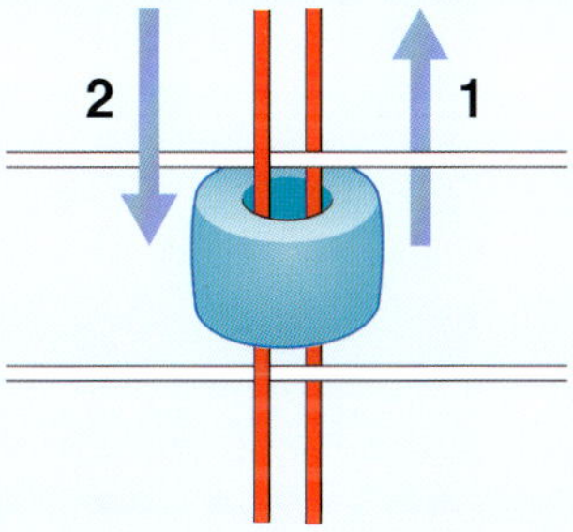

Tip

If the weft thread is too short to continue weaving, pass the remaining thread in a zigzag pattern through the previously woven rows (see step 5). Thread a new weft thread, starting a few rows before the last one and passing again in a zigzag pattern through the previously woven beads. Once the thread reaches the last row, you can continue weaving as normal.

Increasing

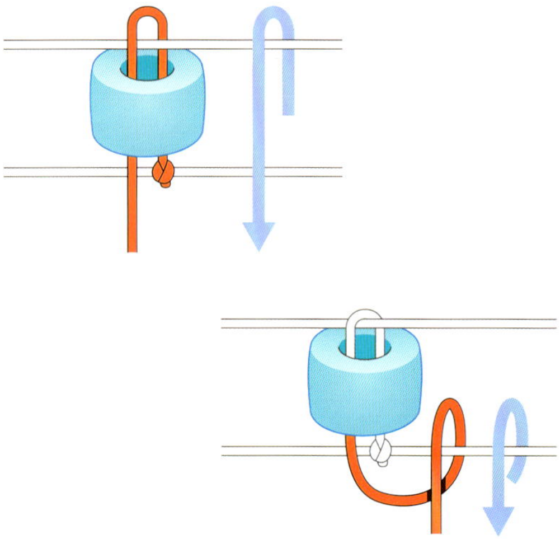

1. Tie the weft thread onto a warp thread. Pick up a bead, then pass the needle and thread back and forth once, as you would for basic weaving. Pass back under and over the warp thread (with the knot) to wrap around it. Tighten to secure the bead. If the first row has several beads, consider this the first bead at the bottom, then thread and weave the other beads in the row as normal.

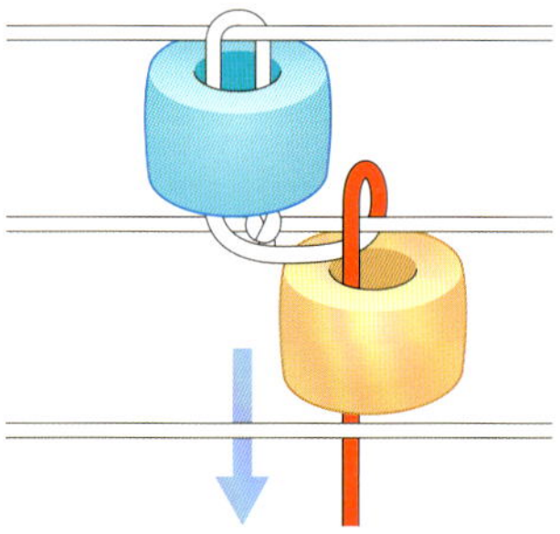

2. Pick up the additional bead in the next row, place it under the warp threads, and hold it in place with your finger. If you have several additional beads, do the same with all of them.

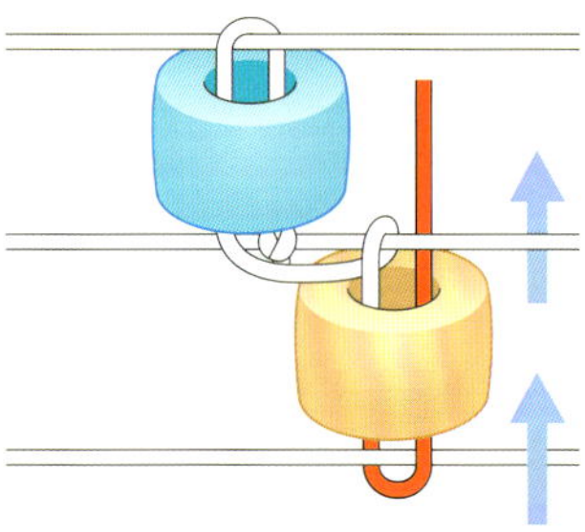

3. Pass the needle over the warp thread (below the bead), through the new bead, and under the warp thread that is above the bead.

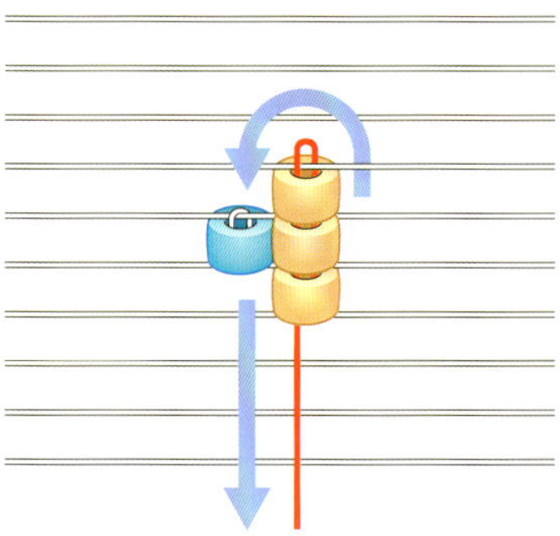

4. Pick up the next beads in this row, placing them under the warp threads. Continue the basic weaving pattern, moving the needle up under the warp threads and down over the threads.

Decreasing

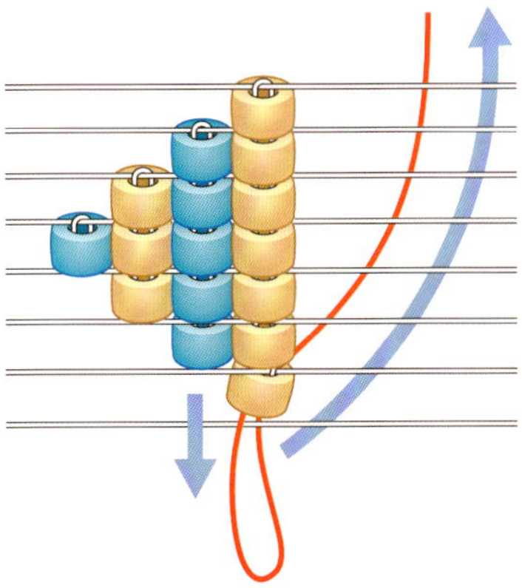

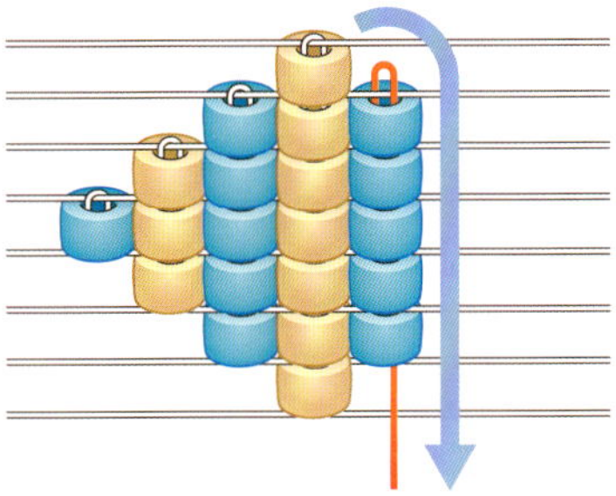

1. To reduce a weaving area, pass the needle through the first woven bead in the last row, passing under the warp threads.

2. Continue weaving as normal.

Finishing with Increases or Decreases

To finish off the weave, pass the thread back through the previous rows in a zigzag pattern. Cut it flush with the bead. Apply dots of glue to the side of each end bead on the warp threads. Once the glue is dry, remove the weave from the loom and cut the excess warp threads flush with the weave.

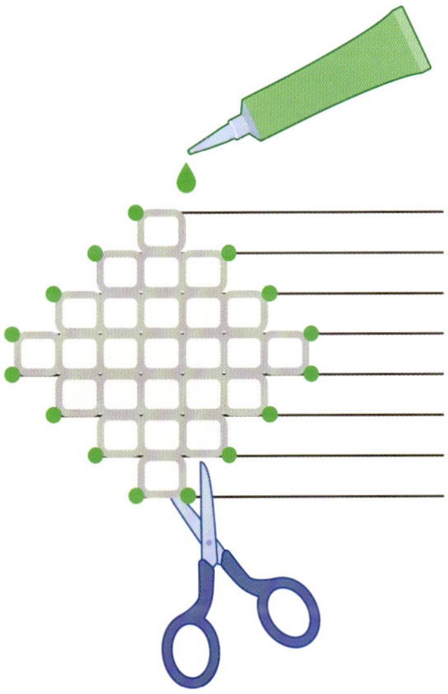

Emerald Ring, page 68

Projects

Cuff Bracelets

Wire-Wrapping Technique

Materials

Miyuki Delica 11/0 beads

Duracoat galvanized gold (DB1832)

Colors of your choice

Gold cuff bracelet

10mm wide

Gold-colored brass wire

Ø = 0.3mm

Diagrams

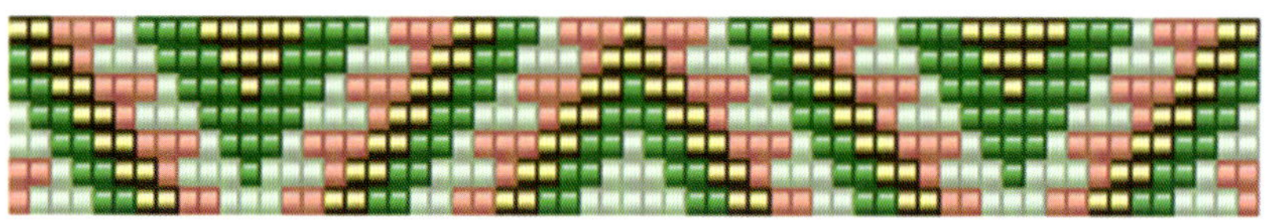

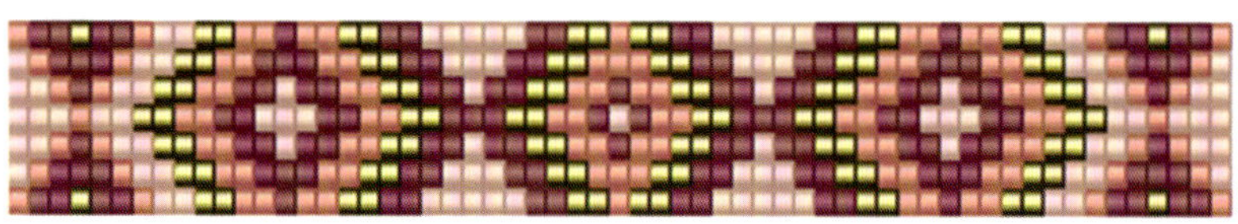

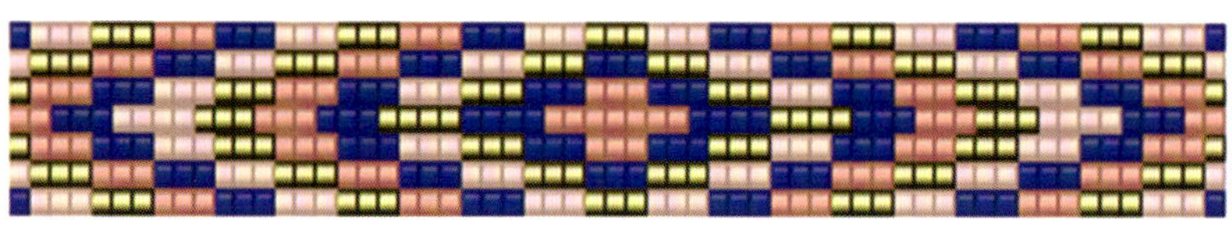

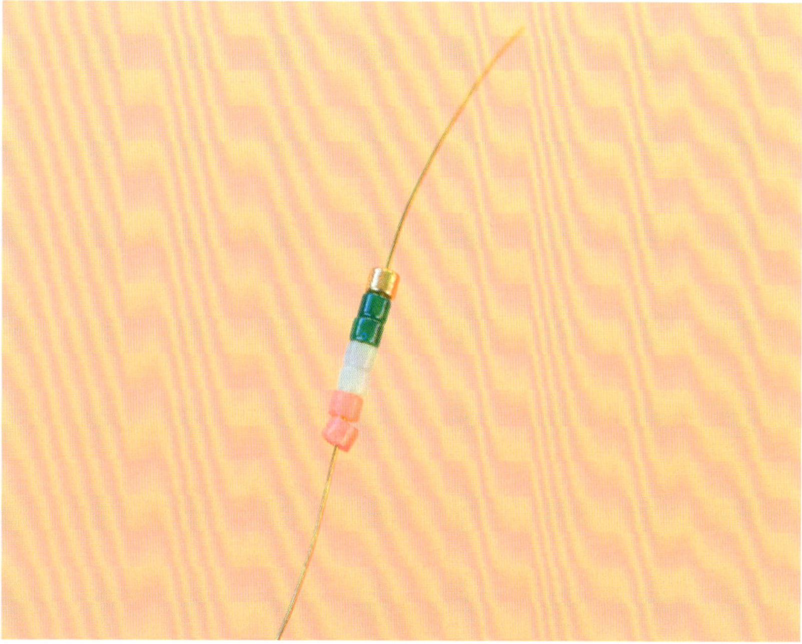

1. Thread the first row of beads onto the brass wire, following the diagram pattern of your choosing. Shown here is the first pattern.

2. Place the beads across the width of the bracelet.

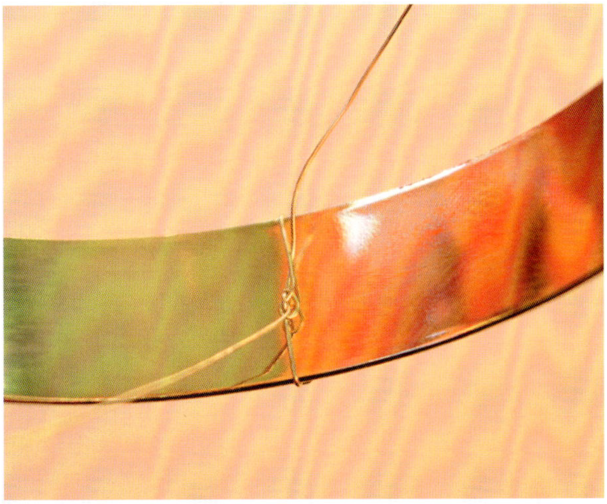

3. Tie a tight double knot at the back of the bracelet. Bring the working wire to the front from the bottom.

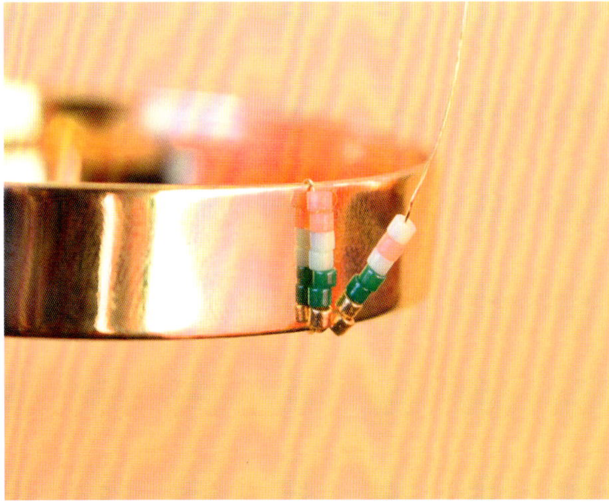

4. Pick up the second row of beads onto the brass wire, following the pattern.

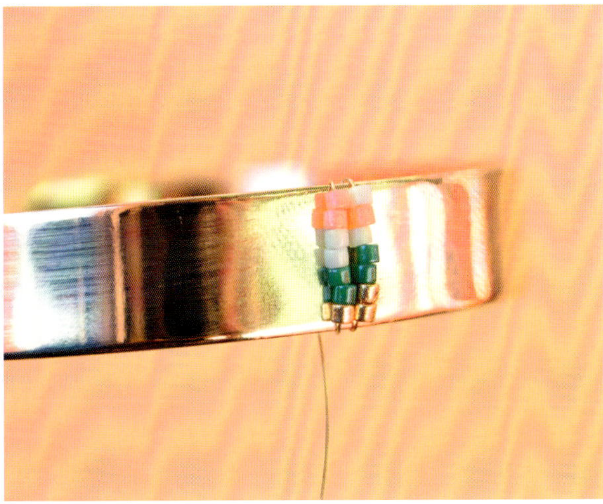

5. Wrap the wire around the width of the bracelet, tucking it over the top to the back.

6. Continue following the pattern. Finish with a knot at the back of the bracelet.

Charleston Earrings

Cross-Weave Technique

Tools and Materials

Miyuki Delica 11/0 beads

Opaque black (DB0010)

Brick red (DB0654)

Duracoat galvanized gold (DB1832)

Gold-colored brass wire

Ø = 0.3mm

Gold chain, approx. 40½" (102.9cm) total

2 lengths of 2¼" (5.7cm)

28 lengths of 1¼" (3.2cm)

2 gold French hook ear wires

Jewelry pliers

Diagram

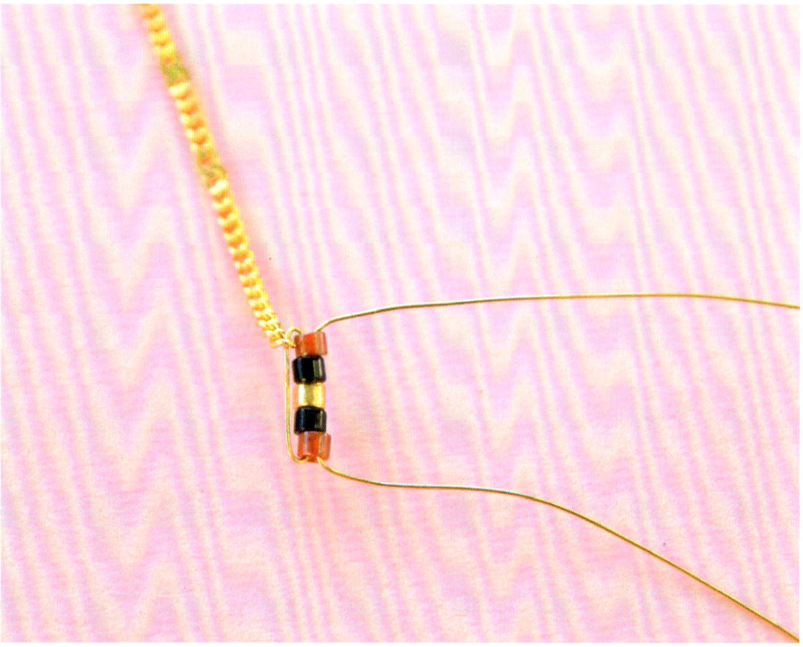

1. Pass a 10" (25.4cm) length of brass wire through the first link of a 2¼" (5.7cm) length of chain, which will join the pendant to the earring hook. Pick up the first row of beads. Pass the other end of the wire through the beads to cross the wires. Tighten to secure them in place.

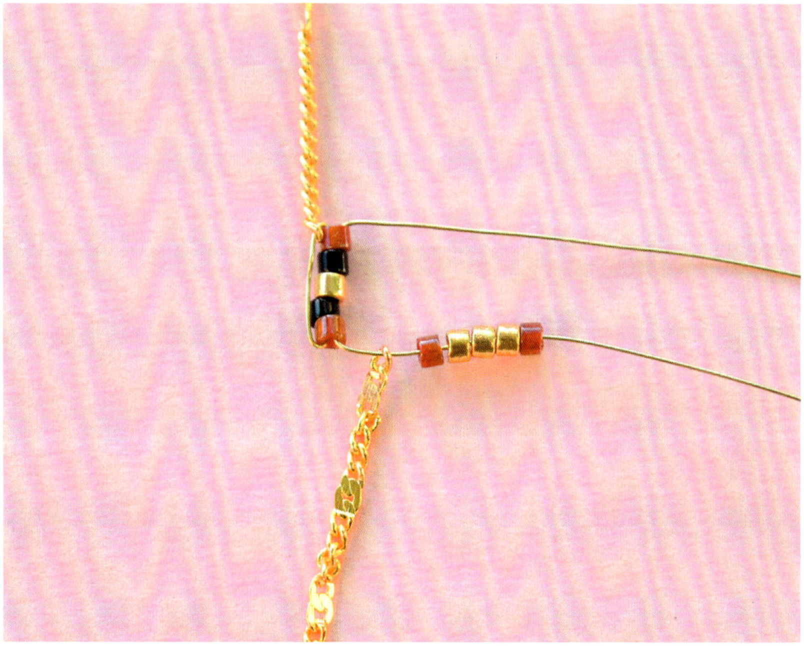

2. Pick up a 1¼" (3.2cm) length of chain with the bottom wire, followed by the beads for the second row.

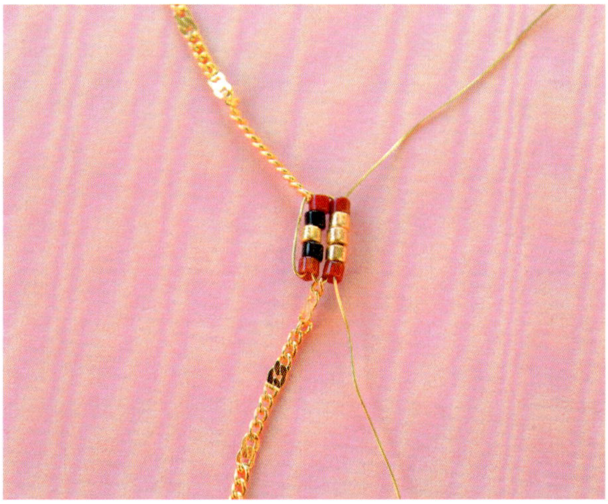

3. Thread the top wire (from step 2) through the second-row beads and tighten.

4. Continue, following the diagram and inserting a small piece of chain between each row. After the last row of beads, pick up the other end of the 2¼" (5.7cm) chain on the brass wire. This connects the pendant to the earring hook.

5. Pass the top wire through the last row of beads. Tighten well and pass the two wires back through the beads in the second-to-last row, crossing them inside as before. Cut the wire flush with the beads.

6. Using pliers, cut the chains into a V shape. Connect the top chain to an earring hook. Use a jump ring if needed. Repeat for the second earring.

Portobello Road Necklace

Odd-Count Peyote Stitch

Tools and Materials

Miyuki Delica 11/0 beads

Opaque white (DB0200)

Opaque glass enamel light mint (DB1496)

Opaque salmon (DB1363)

Opaque matte agate blue (DB1587)

Duracoat opaque dyed light lemon ice (DB2101)

Duracoat galvanized gold (DB1832)

Beading thread

Beading needle

Gold chain, approx. 23½" (59.7cm) total

2 lengths of 11¾" (29.8cm)

4 small jump rings

Ø = 2 or 3mm

Lobster clasp and jump ring

Ø = 5mm

Extra-strong glue

Jewelry pliers

Diagram

1. Weave the rectangular base of the houses in odd-count peyote stitch (see page 12) according to the diagram pattern.

2. Once the base is complete, each roof must be woven separately. Let's use the green house as an example: Pull the thread out from the last bead on the top right of the golden house. Pass the needle diagonally through the first two beads of the green house.

3. Pick up a bead, then pass the needle through the bead to the right of the first two.

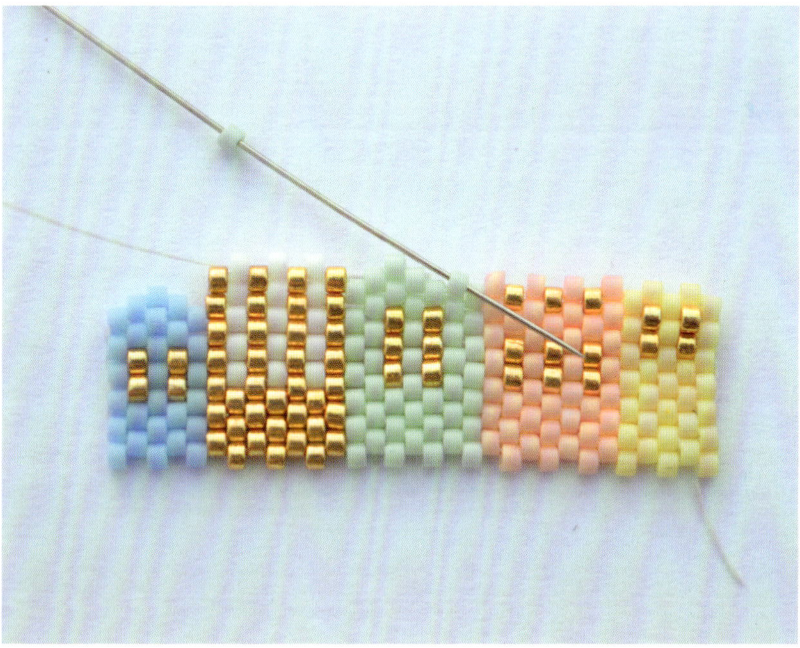

4. As before, pick up a bead and then pass the needle through the bead on its right.

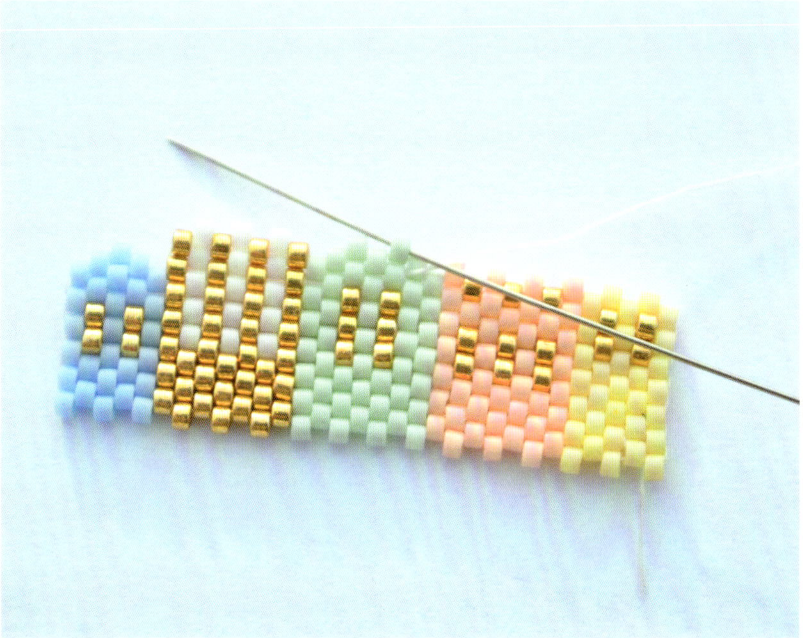

5. To decrease, pass the needle through the previously woven beads, so that the needle comes out of the top bead. Pick up a bead and pass the needle through the bead on the left (final base row) to finish the roof of the house.

6. Zigzag the needle through the previously woven beads, finally pulling the thread out of the first bead of the next house.

7. Continue weaving the roof of the next house in peyote stitch all the way to the top, then move on to the other houses.

8. To finish, pass the needle through the woven beads in a random zigzag pattern. Apply a dot of glue to the thread. Once the glue is dry, cut the thread flush with the bead.

9. Using small jump rings, connect a length of chain on each side. Then connect the ends of the chain to the clasp and the 5mm jump ring.

Diamonds Bracelet

Odd-Count Peyote Stitch

Tools and Materials

Miyuki Delica 11/0 beads

Opaque glass enamel light mint (DB1496)

Duracoat semi-frosted silver-lined matte dyed spearmint (DB2188)

Opaque green (DB0656)

Duracoat galvanized gold (DB1832)

Beading thread

Beading needle

2 small jump rings

Ø = 2 or 3mm

Lobster clasp and jump ring

Ø = 5mm

Extra-strong glue

Jewelry pliers

Diagram

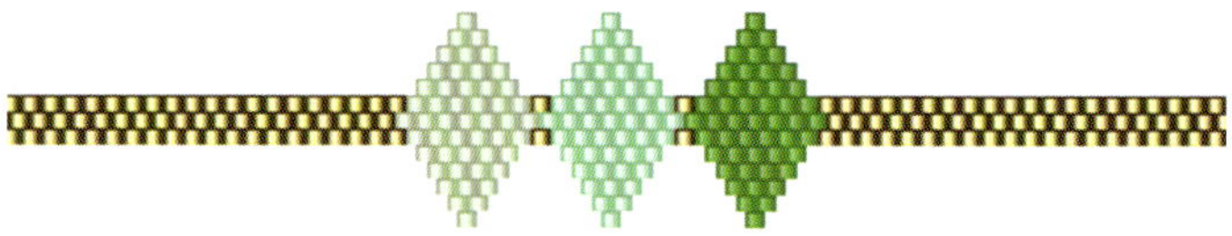

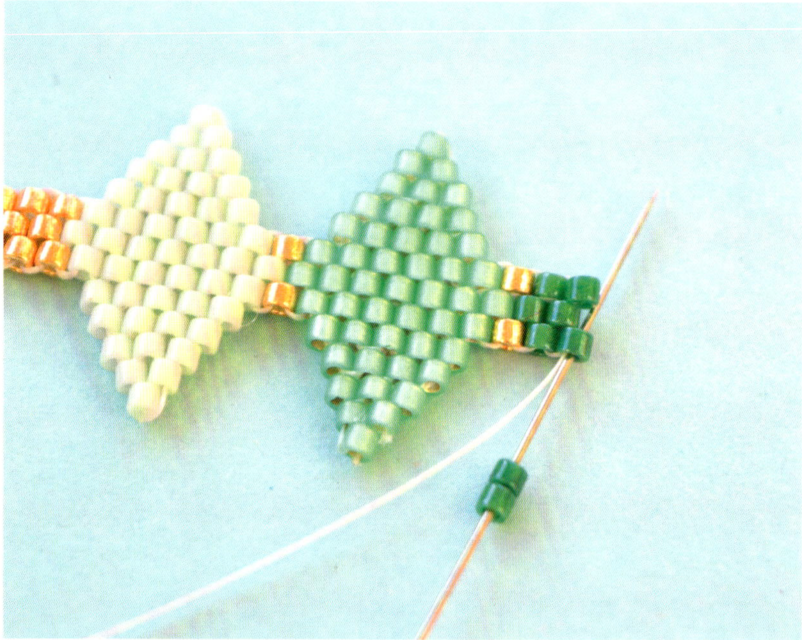

1. Weave the first gold part of the bracelet using odd-count peyote stitch (see page 12). For the diamonds, the dark green will serve as an example for the technique used in all three diamonds. Weave the first four rows in odd-count peyote (only work: one bead, two beads, one bead, two beads). Pick up two beads and pass the needle back through the bead that the thread comes out of.

2. Tighten the thread so the two beads sit side by side. Pick up a bead and pass the needle through the top bead.

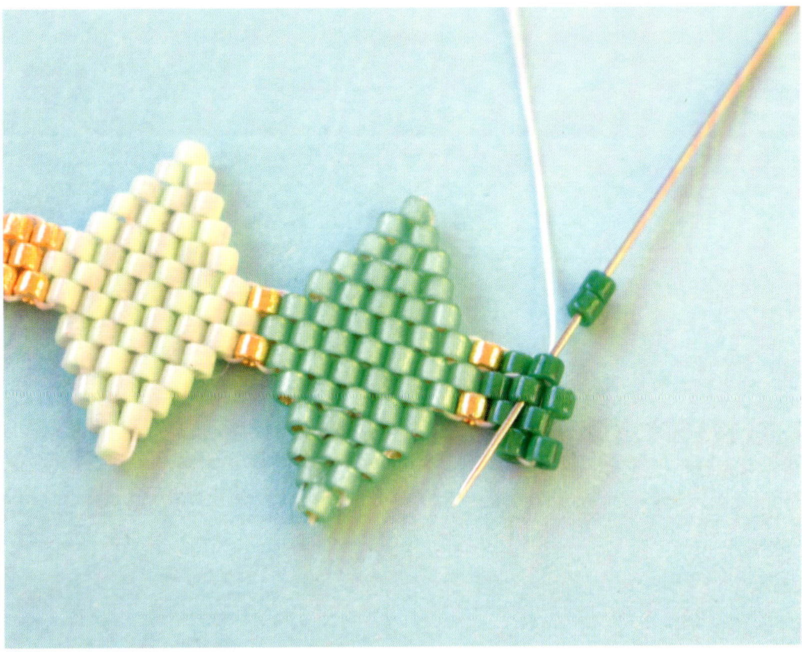

3. To increase at the top, pick up two beads and pass the needle back through the bead that the thread comes out of, then through the bead below it.

4. Tighten the thread until the beads sit side by side, then pass the needle diagonally back through three beads.

5. Pass the needle back through the top-right bead.

6. Continue weaving as normal.

7. Once at the top of the diamond, decrease symmetrically (see Decreasing for Even or Odd Peyote on page 13). Continue weaving the bracelet with gold beads.

8. To finish, pass the needle through the woven beads in a random zigzag pattern. Apply a dot of glue to the thread. Once the glue is dry, cut the thread flush with the bead. Connect the bracelet to the clasp and the 5mm jump ring using the two small jump rings.

Multicolored Hoops

Brick Stitch

Tools and Materials

Miyuki Delica 11/0 beads

Opaque matte cyan blue (DB1588)

Opaque matte turquoise green (DB0759)

Opaque red (DB0723)

Opaque yellow (DB721)

Opaque salmon (DB1363)

Duracoat galvanized gold (DB1832)

Beading thread

Beading needle

2 gold hoop ear wires with crimp closures

Ø = 30mm

2 gold French hook ear wires

Extra-strong glue

Scissors

Diagram

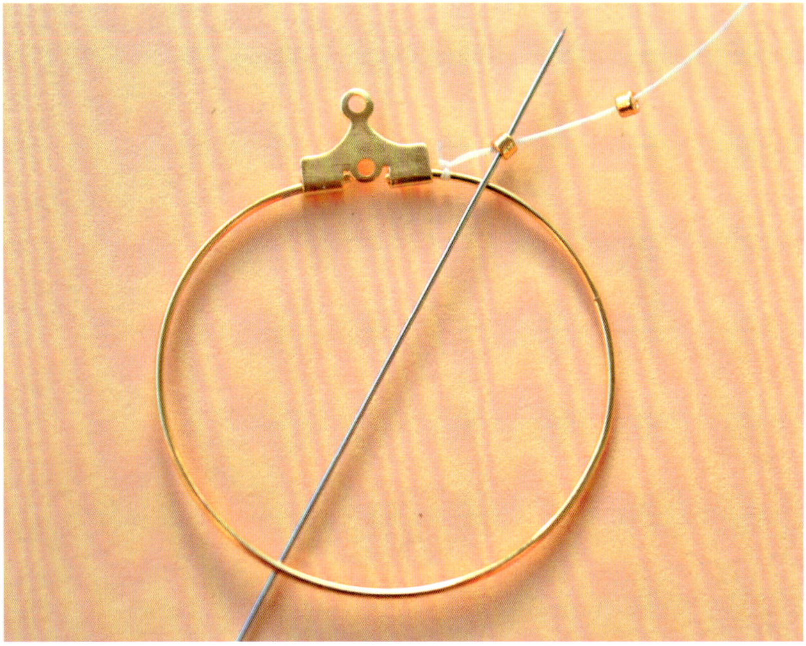

1. Tie a long piece of thread securely to the hoop. Pick up the first two beads, then pass the needle from the bottom over the hoop then up through the first bead.

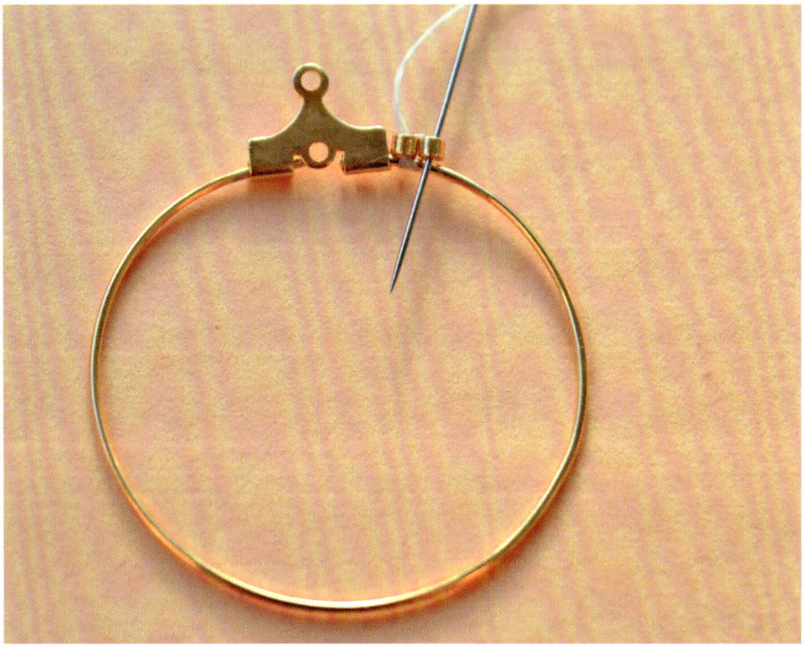

2. Tighten the thread so the beads are positioned correctly. Pass the needle from the top down through the second bead, in front of the hoop.

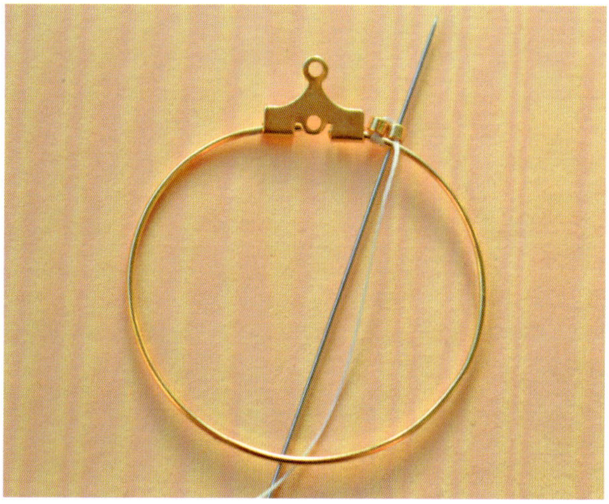

3. Pass the needle back through the same bead in the opposite direction, but this time behind the hoop.

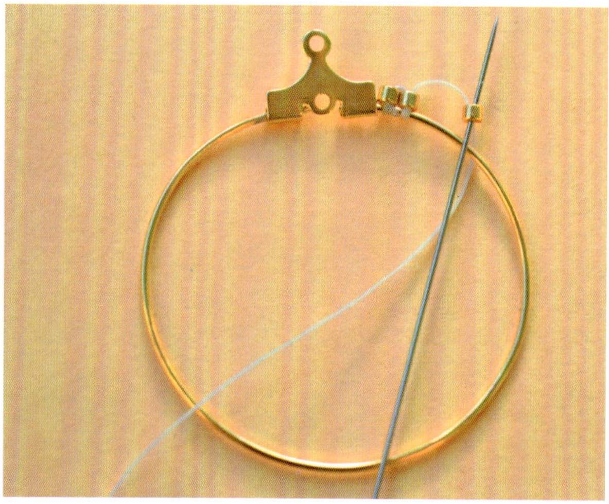

4. Pick up another bead, staying behind the hoop. Pass the needle back through the same bead, keeping in front of the hoop. Tighten the thread to position the bead.

5. Continue this first row as in the previous steps around the entire hoop. At the end of the row, zigzag the thread through the previously woven beads. Apply a dot of glue to the thread. Once the glue is dry, cut the thread flush with the bead.

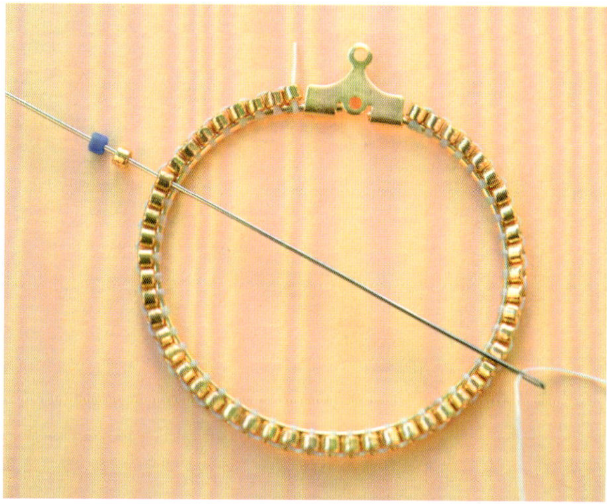

6. For the second row, use a new length of thread. Pass the needle through the tenth bead (photo shows the ninth bead) from the top left, and pick up the first two beads in the pattern.

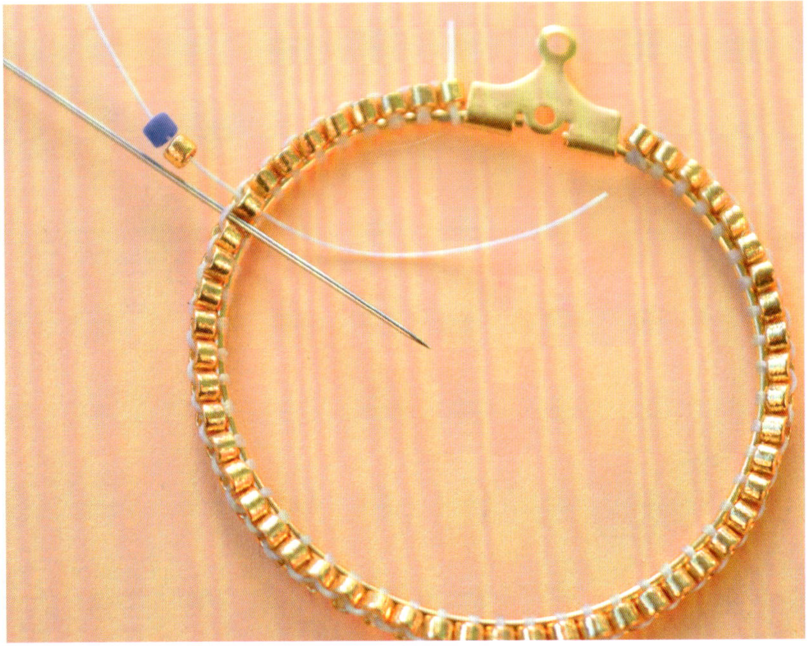

7. Do a basic brick stitch (see page 16) by sliding the needle under the thread bridge that joins the tenth and eleventh beads (photo shows ninth and tenth).

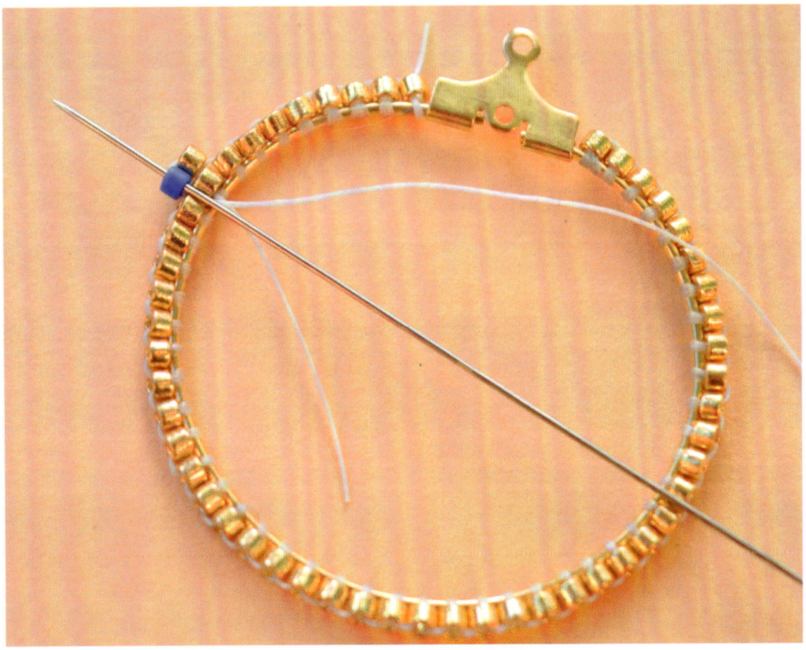

8. Pass the needle up through the second bead.

9. Continue in brick stitch to complete each row according to the diagram.

10. To finish, pass the needle through the woven beads in a random zigzag pattern. Apply a dot of glue to the thread. Once the glue is dry, cut the thread flush with the bead. Attach the hoop to an earring hook. Repeat for the second earring.

Brooch Medley

Loom Technique

Tools and Materials

Miyuki Delica 11/0 beads
Colors of your choice

Weaving loom

Nylon thread
Weft threads: Ø = 0.1mm
Warp threads: Ø = 0.25mm

Beading needle

Bar pin backs

Extra-strong glue

Jewelry glue

Diagrams

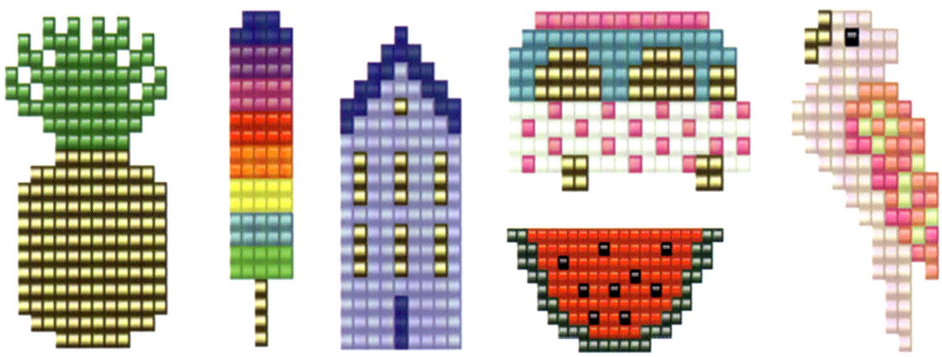

1. Weave the chosen diagram pattern on a loom (see page 20). Zigzag the 0.1mm weft thread into the previously woven beads. Apply extra-strong glue all around the pattern on the threads. Once the glue is dry, cut the threads flush with the beads.

2. Glue a bar pin to the back using jewelry glue. Allow to dry thoroughly before wearing the brooch.

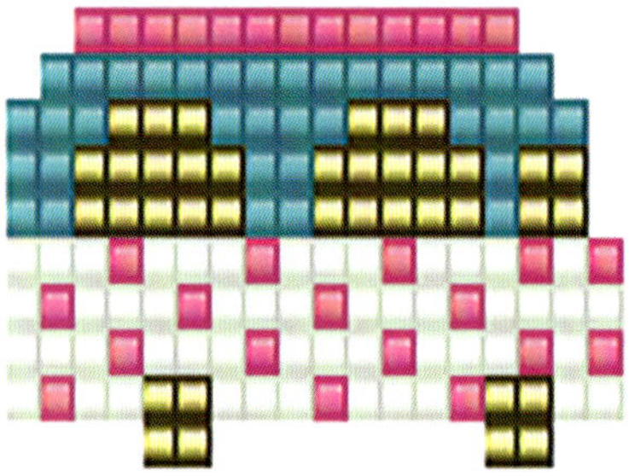

Have fun with colors in this project! These brooches can easily be customized as desired or you can let beads in your stash lead you to something new.

Cobalt Bracelet

Loom Technique

Tools and Materials

Miyuki Delica 11/0 beads

Duracoat galvanized gold (DB1832)

Opaque matte agate blue (DB1587)

Opaque matte cyan blue (DB1588)

Weaving loom

Nylon thread

Weft threads: Ø = 0.1mm

Warp threads: Ø = 0.25mm

Beading needle

2 small jump rings

Ø = 2 or 3mm

Lobster clasp and jump ring

Ø = 5mm

Extra-strong glue

Diagram

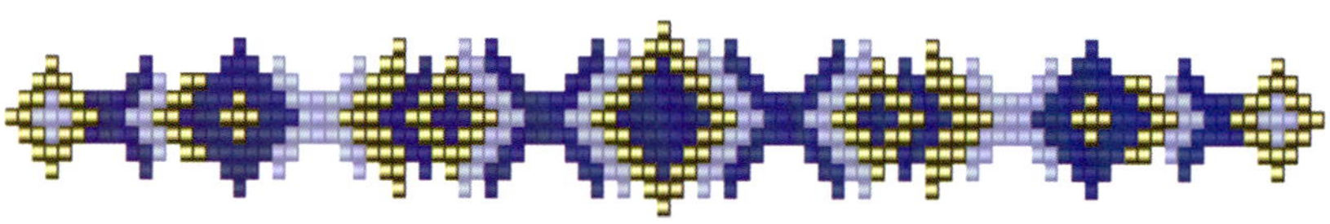

1. Stretch and secure 10 strands of 0.25mm warp thread on the loom. Tie a long piece of 0.1mm weft thread to the fifth warp thread from the bottom.

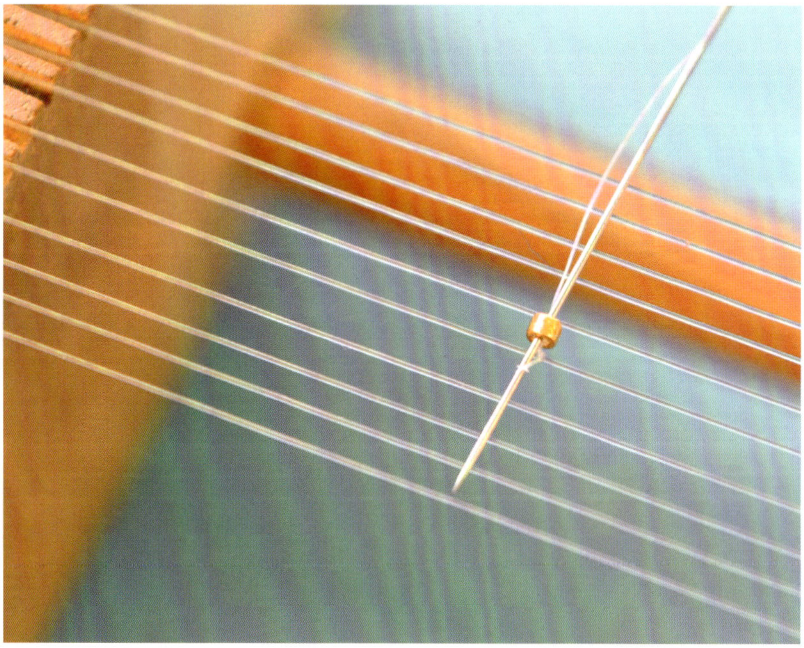

2. Pick up the first bead and secure it under the warp threads using your finger. Pass the needle through the bead from top to bottom, making sure it goes over the warp threads.

3. To increase the weaving area, pass the needle from bottom to top under the thread on which the first bead is located (the fifth from the bottom).

4. Wrap around the warp thread so the needle is back the bottom. Pull the weft thread tight.

5. Pick up the second bead, place it under the warp threads, and pass the needle from bottom to top, overtop the warp threads.

6. Pick up the next two beads under the warp threads, then pass the needle from top to bottom through all the beads, including the very first one, taking care to go on top of the warp threads this time. Continue like this for the next two rows.

7. To decrease the weaving area, pass the needle from bottom to top through the first woven bead of the last row, with the thread under the warp threads.

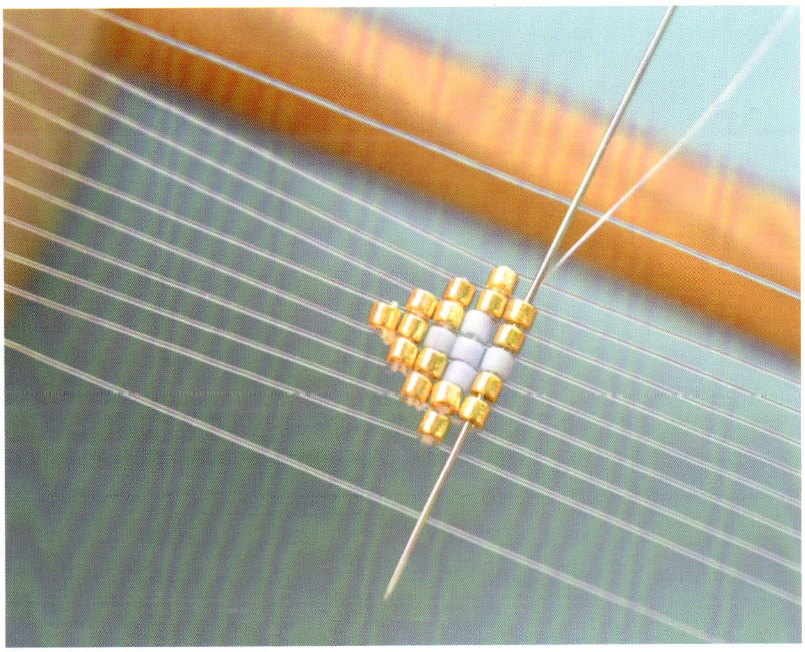

8. Continue weaving, following the same methods.

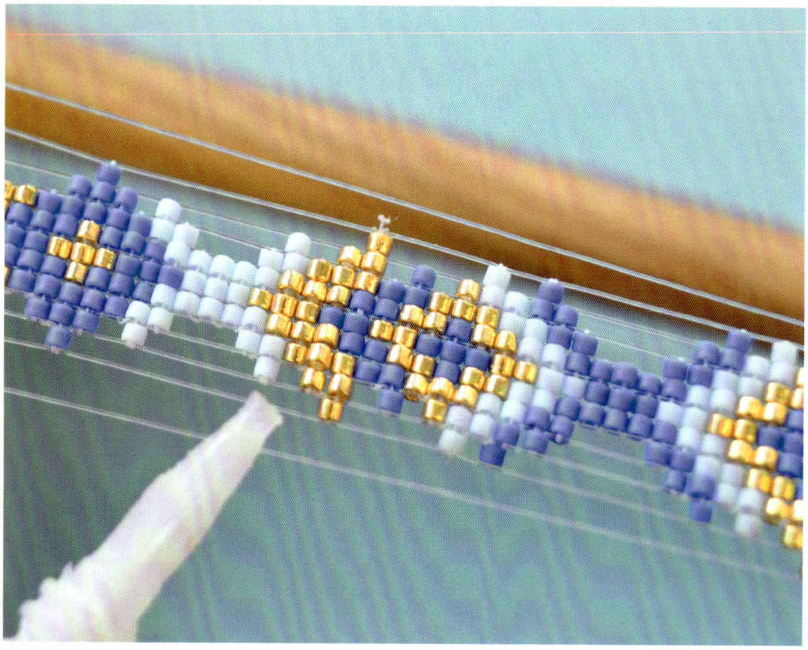

9. Once you've finished weaving, zigzag the thread through the previously woven beads. Apply dots of glue to the threads all around the bracelet.

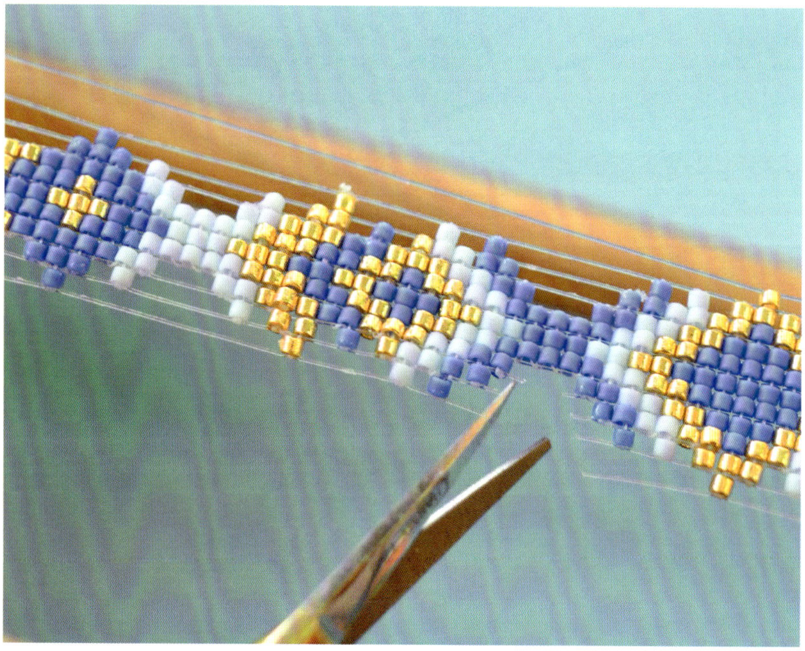

10. Once the glue is completely dry, cut the warp wires flush with the beads.

11. Detach the bracelet from the loom and attach a small jump ring to the end bead on each side of the bracelet. Connect one small jump ring to the clasp and the other to the 5mm jump ring and clasp.

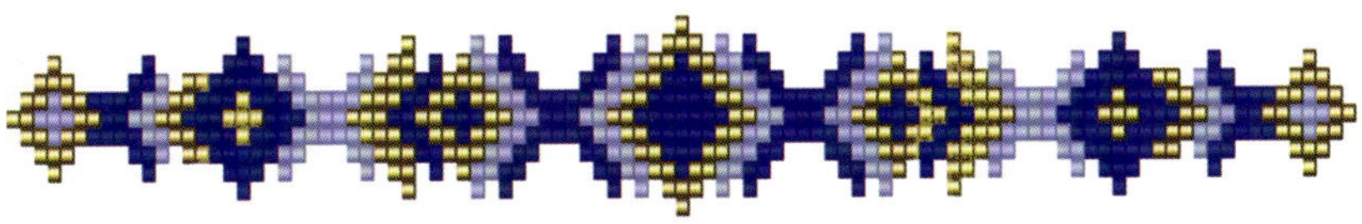

Bird on a Perch Necklace

Brick Stitch

Tools and Materials

Bird: Miyuki Delica 11/0 beads

Opaque white (DB0200)

Opaque salmon (DB1363)

Opaque avocado (DB1135)

Matte opaque sea foam luster (DB0374)

Opaque black (DB0010)

Dark cotton candy pink Ceylon (DB0246)

Dyed opaque squash (DB0651)

Leaves: Miyuki Delica 11/0 beads

Matte opaque green (DB0754)

Beading thread

Beading needle

Gold hoop ear wire with crimp closure

Ø = 40mm

Gold chain

Approx. 19¾" (50.2cm)

2 small jump rings

Ø = 2 or 3mm

Lobster clasp and jump ring

Ø = 5mm

Extra-strong glue

Jewelry pliers

Diagrams

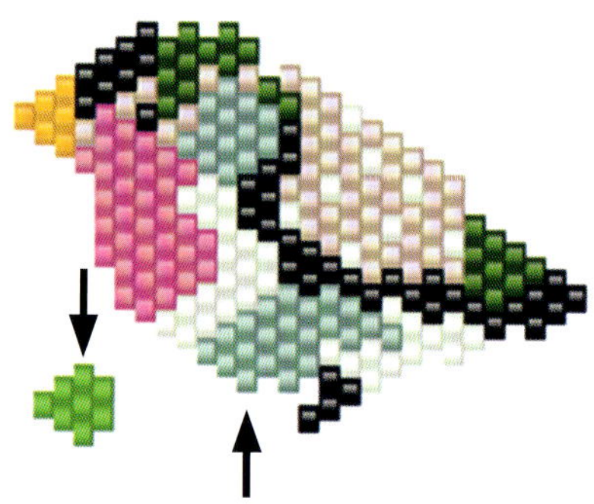

1. Weave each element using brick stitch (see page 16), starting at the arrows in the diagram. Make five leaves or as many as desired. To finish, zigzag the thread through the previously woven beads. Apply a dot of glue to the thread. Once the glue is dry, cut the thread flush with the bead.

2. Open the hoop. Pick up three leaves through their top bead. Then pick up the bird through the bead that forms its foot, centering it on the hoop. Using a needle and thread, attach the bird's beak and tail to the hoop, winding the thread around the wire and tying a knot at the end.

3. Pick up the last two leaves and close the hoop using flat pliers. Apply a dot of glue to keep the leaves in place.

4. Thread the chain through the hoop, then attach one end to the clasp and the other to the 5mm ring.

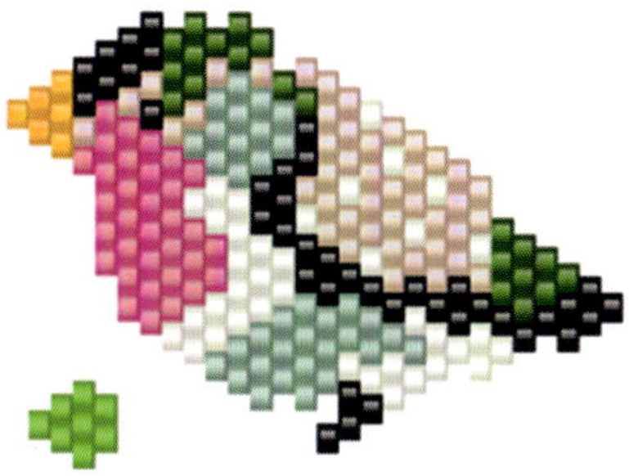

Emerald Ring

Circular Peyote Stitch

Tools and Materials

Miyuki Delica 11/0 beads

Duracoat galvanized gold (DB1832)

Matte transparent dark emerald (DB0767)

Beading thread

Beading needle

Diagram

Measure your middle knuckle (the widest part of your finger) using a tape measure to determine the ring size you need. Adjust the diagram accordingly. A finger circumference of 2¼" (5.7cm) has been used for this diagram.

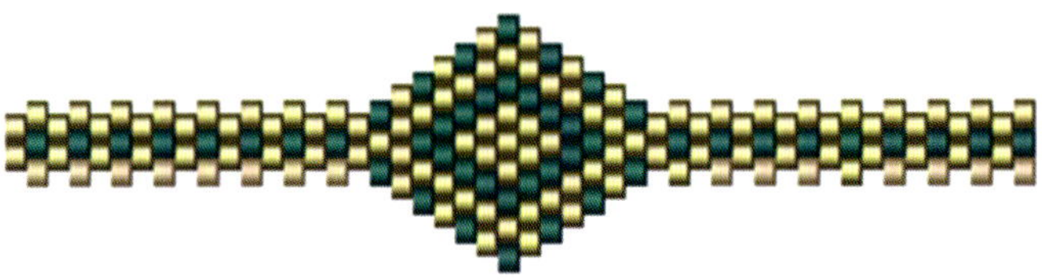

1. Weave the five rows that make up the body of the ring using circular peyote (see page 14), as shown in the diagram. Pass the needle through the gold bead directly above the tip of the green diamond, and begin weaving the upper part of the diamond.

2. Once you have woven the first row of the upper part of the diamond, pass the needle from left to right through the beads you've just woven . . .

3. . . . and then pass it from right to left to pull it out through the last bead in the first row of the diamond. Begin weaving the second row of the upper part using the even-count peyote stitch (see page 11).

4. Continue weaving the upper part of the ring head, following steps 2 and 3 to move from one row to the next.

5. Once the upper part is finished, pass the needle and thread through the previously woven beads to the lower part of the diamond.

6. Weave the lower part in the same way as the upper part. To finish, zigzag the thread through the woven beads, then apply a dot of glue to the thread. Once the glue is dry, cut the thread flush with the bead.

Harlequin Bracelet

Circular Peyote Stitch

Tools and Materials

Miyuki Delica 11/0 beads

Duracoat galvanized gold (DB1832)

Antique ivory silk satin (DB0673)

Opaque cobalt blue (DB0726)

Opaque green (DB0656)

Duracoat dyed opaque columbine (DB2138)

Opaque turquoise green (DB0658)

Opaque light salmon (DB1493)

Duracoat opaque lychee (DB2113)

Beading thread

Beading needle

Diagram

Measure the circumference of your hand (see page 14) to determine the bracelet size you need. Adjust the diagram accordingly. A circumference of 8" (20.3cm) has been used for this diagram.

1. Pick up the beads for the first and second rows alternately (see page 14) onto a strand of thread approximately 6½ feet (2m) in length.

2. Pass the needle back through the first bead so that the threads cross, then pull the thread to form the bracelet.

3. Start the third row: pick up the first bead, then pass the thread through the second bead for the second row, skipping the first bead for the first row.

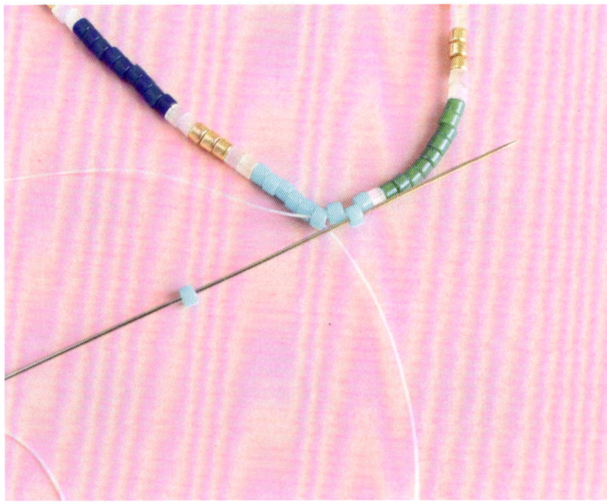

4. Continue the row using the even-count peyote stitch (see page 11).

5. When you get to the end of the row, pick up the last bead for the third row and . . .

6. . . . start the fourth row by passing the needle back through the first bead in the third row. Follow this method to weave this and subsequent rows. To finish, zigzag the thread through the previously woven beads, then apply a dot of glue to the thread. Once the glue is dry, cut the thread flush with the bead.

Lone Cloud Necklace

Brick Stitch

Tools and Materials

Cloud: Miyuki Delica 11/0 beads

Silver lined crystal (DB0041)

Crystal AB white silk satin (DB0670)

Crystal Ceylon white (DB0231)

Raindrops: Miyuki Delica 11/0 beads

Opaque salmon (DB1363)

Opaque green (DB0656)

Opaque glass enamel light mint (DB1496)

Matte opaque sea foam luster (DB0374)

Opaque light salmon (DB1493)

Beading thread

Beading needle

Gold chain, approx. 27½" (69.9cm) total

2 lengths of 1¾" (4.4cm)

2 lengths of ¾" (1.9cm)

1 length of 1" (2.5cm)

2 lengths of 10¾" (27.3cm)

Lobster clasp and jump ring

Ø = 5mm

4 small jump rings

Ø = 2 or 3mm

Extra-strong glue

Jewelry pliers

Diagrams

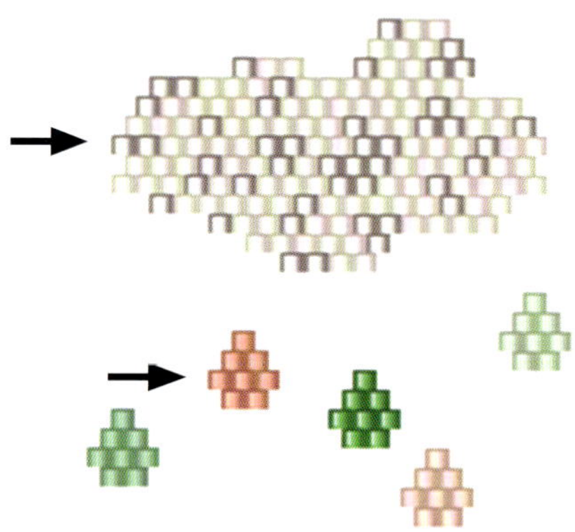

1. Weave each element using brick stitch (see page 16), starting at the arrows in the diagrams. Finally, zigzag the thread through the woven beads. Apply a dot of glue to the thread. Once the glue is dry, cut the thread flush with the bead.

2. To attach each raindrop, pass the thread through the beads from bottom to top. Pick up the first link of a length of chain and pass back through the beads from top to bottom. Tighten to secure the raindrop to the chain. Apply a dot of glue where the thread comes out. Once the glue is dry, cut the thread. Repeat for each raindrop.

3. Where the first raindrop will hang, pass a new thread from the top of the cloud to the bottom, then pick up the first link of the chain (opposite end from the raindrop). Pull the thread tight.

4. For the next raindrop, pass the thread from top to bottom through the cloud. Secure each raindrop with the same thread. To finish, zigzag through the cloud and apply a dot of glue. Once the glue is dry, cut the thread flush with the bead. Attach each side of the cloud to a chain with a small jump ring. Attach one end of the chain to the 5mm jump ring and the other to the clasp.

Index

Note: Page numbers in *italics* indicate projects.